FOOD & FAITH

WENDY WHITESIDE

with Leader's Guide by FAYE WILSON

FOOD & FAITH

WENDY WHITESIDE

with Leader's Guide by FAYE WILSON

Women's Division • The General Board of Global Ministries
The United Methodist Church

ISBN 978-1-933663-32-6
Library of Congress Control Number: 2008932380
Printed in the United States of America

CONTENTS

INTRODUCTION

As Christians, faith is a central part of our lives. Faith strengthens us. The knowledge that Christ is with us—we are not alone—gives us confidence to face the everyday and the extraordinary. Faith comforts us. The promise that God loves us and will not leave us comfortless sustains us in every situation. Faith guides us. The blessings, bounty, love, strength, and comfort through our faith in God, Christ, and the Holy Spirit require a response. It requires thanks and sharing. These responses are not just found in worship. Opportunities to offer God's love, share Christ's grace, and show the blessings of the Holy Spirit to others are all ways in which to actively respond to God's abundant love.

Our faith is nurtured through the scriptures, prayer, and ritual. This is where we meet God and relate to the divine. But we think too narrowly if these are the only situations or activities where we recognize our connection to God. God is with us always and seeking to interact with us every moment.

In this book we will explore how our faith is nurtured, strengthened, and enhanced, by food and all the ways food touches our lives.

Food is such an ordinary thing. We need it daily to survive and thrive. It is so ubiquitous that we plan our lives around eating. No matter how busy our lives get, food finds a place in our schedules—breakfast, lunch, dinner, and snacks. But the very fact that we need to eat about three times a day (or so our mothers told us) has led most of us to take food for granted. Our cabinets are stocked and there are many restaurants, and so feeding ourselves and our loved ones has become something to fit into our days. A meal is a goal, a target to aim for, so that we can multitask. A meal is a twofer: fuel and a meeting; fuel and a moment to see your family; fuel and your favorite TV show.

And yet food is a gift from God. It represents God's love for us. This wonderful world that God created provides us with all that we need to live—air, water, food, shelter—the basic elements a person needs to live and function. It is no accident that our most profound sacrament, Holy Communion, is food. In chapter one, we discuss just how the bread and fruit of the vine illustrate the magnitude of God's love for us on multiple levels.

The act of Holy Communion is a means of grace. In this sacrament we find a place where God offers each of us, in tangible ways, a channel for receiving God's grace. It is a sacred act that brings the supplicant and the maker into direct, material communion. God's presence is invoked and the divine and the ordinary connect in a mystery created by Christ and ordained by God. In this way, we are reminded that the food we eat is a gift of God. We are reminded that the connection between God's presence in our lives and our physical sustenance is an intimate one and not to be ignored.

The presence of God in our lives is shared in community when the faithful gather for sustenance in the form of fellowship and food. It is an extension of the Communion table when the church family gathers around coffee and cookies, a benefit dinner, a meal of celebration, or in many other ways. Food is never far from a gathering of the faithful.

When we partake of nourishment, a word of thanks reminds us of the ready presence of God. A prayer, a personal moment of reflection, a public expression of gratitude for the bounty we enjoy from God, give us a chance to remember just how near God is. We remember God's eternal love for us manifest in the food we eat.

Chapter two moves us to explore the ways in which we involve food in our lives. Our daily interaction with food takes all forms. The fast pace at which we live our lives sometimes reduces the food we eat to fuel, making our interactions with food a means to an end. Food is necessary. It allows us to meet all the physical, emotional, and mental responsibilities and desires we have. It is a tool to be used, a necessity to be met.

Food can also be a companion; a comforter; a quiet, friendly presence that can fill empty moments in our lives. Through food we try to take in the fullness of life. In this form, food is used to nourish the hunger that many feel, which cannot be assuaged by purely physical means.

For others food is the enemy. It is a cruel addiction that must be managed, controlled, and overcome. Food meant to nourish and sustain is scorned and we waste away from unappeased want.

Our relationships with food are complex and individual just as our relationships are with God. As we discover in the first chapter the deep and abiding connection between food and faith, we try in this chapter to find ways of bringing God into our everyday relationship with food. Living our faith in all the aspects of our lives can lead to healing, growth, and a deepening relationship with God.

The relationship between food and faith is also found in our hospitality to others. In chapter three, we explore the biblical imperative to offer hospitality—to our friends and to the stranger. In Greek, the word for hospitality is *philoxenos*— a combination of *philo* (love) and *xenos* (stranger). This is the same kind of love (*philo*) offered to Jesus by the woman or stranger (*xenos*) who bathed his feet and anointed them with her tears in Luke. It is the act of moving beyond oneself for another. This is the kind of hospitality we discover in this book. Hospitality has deep, profound meaning for our spiritual lives and is more than a simple offering of refreshment to a neighbor.

It is in this chapter on hospitality that we delve into the places where our own spiritual growth evolves into an outward demonstration of our faith and God's love to others. Our personal relationship with God is often what we mean when we focus on spiritual development. Here we stretch the personal component of our faith lives and expand our circle even wider, showing the depth and breadth of our faith experience through the respect and nourishment of others. Food allows us to do this. Food, the bread of life, embodies our faithful response to move into the world.

Finally, the rituals of feasting and fasting remind us of our need for God. The feasting that we engage in around moments of celebration and praise fills us with God's goodness. The act of joyfully acknowledging the fullness of God's creation in a feast— either implicitly or explicitly—adds spiritual nourishment to the physical and emotional nourishment abundant in such gatherings. This is as true now as in the days of King David.

Fasting, an ancient ritual of submissive cleansing of the soul and body, is a very real reminder of our dependence on God's love and grace. While this ritual is not embraced by the US culture, it does offer an important opportunity to more completely embrace God's generosity by refraining from the most basic physical gift for a short time. This chapter gives information on reasons to fast, and healthy ways to fast and grow from the ritual of fasting.

The nourishment that God gives physically and spiritually can be found in abundance and in scarcity. We have Wesley's words to remind us that we can be both empty and full for God. "Let me be full, let me be empty. Let me have all things, let me have nothing."[1] This final chapter tells us that when we can take the time to explore the spiritual benefits of being full or empty, the food given to us by God for our well-being will satisfy more completely.

The relationship between food and faith is often overlooked by those of us who live in the US culture. It is an almost subliminal connection that we only recognize when we are confronted with a book such as this. I hope that you will take the time to reflect on the ways in which food forms and frames your faith journey. I hope you will begin to recognize the glorious, mysterious link between faith and food in your life. Take a moment and praise God for the ever-present gift of life and love that food is for each of us.

CHAPTER 1

Bread of Life

I love food! I think that food is one of the best gifts that God has given humanity. Food is life. It is joy, delight, and comfort. Food comes in all shapes, flavors, colors, and seasons. Food is sweet and spicy, hot and cold, rich and light, coarse and smooth, liquid and solid, hard and soft, juicy and dry, tangy and mild, and so much more. All this food—in all its varieties—comes from God.

God created us to enjoy food. It delights the senses. The aromas of food entice us. They evoke memories of previous encounters, events, and relationships. The colors and shapes that accompany aroma are an invitation to taste and savor. We relish taste, texture, and consistency. It is enjoyable, satisfying, delightful, gratifying. Food is not just fuel for the body; it is much more, and it is more by divine design.

God wants us to enjoy our lives. When our basic needs are met—as God has crafted our bodies and our souls—they are satisfying. Our most basic needs of food, shelter, and water fill us with pleasure and security. When we have been out in cold weather and return to a warm home, gratitude rises from us like steam. When our throats and tongues are dry and parched, a glass of water spreads delight throughout our bodies. Words of praise and thanksgiving erupt from our mouths when our appetite is satisfied by a juicy, ripe peach straight from the tree.

This great gift of food is a tangible symbol of God's presence in our lives. In our drive to satisfy our hunger, food occupies our thoughts throughout the day. This nourishment is enriched as we recognize its source. Our need is more deeply satisfied when we acknowledge God's gift.

Our hunger for food is a true reflection of our hunger for God. Food is the basis of our physical lives, just as our relationship with God is the basis of our spiritual life. As food brings us joy, so does our faith in God. This is not just a handy metaphor, for without God's great love and care for humanity our hungers and desires would not find fulfillment.

In Christ both physical and spiritual food are unified. Jesus, in the Gospel According to John, says, "I am the bread of life. Whoever comes to me will never be hungry, and whoever believes in me will never be thirsty" (John 6:35).

What an extravagant offer! Jesus offers to feed, nourish, refresh, and sustain us. The daily struggle for sustenance will be eased. The people of his day were overwhelmed by this statement. Even today we stand in awe of such remarkable generosity. The joy and the satisfaction we experience in eating is available to us for eternity through Christ Jesus.

Jesus offers us a place at the table by offering to eat with us. When we accept Christ's invitation, we find fellowship with God. When we eat with Christ our souls are satisfied. The food we eat in the presence of Christ fills a space deeper than physical hunger. We take God into ourselves as we take in the food; we commune with God.

Communion

With every meal we commune with God. We commemorate our deep and abiding dependence on God for all our needs, for all our joy, for all our strength. Nowhere is this dependence more fully witnessed than in the sacrament of Holy Communion.

The sacrament of Holy Communion is known by many

names: Mass, the Divine Liturgy, the Eucharist, the Lord's Supper, and—in the early church—it was referred to as "breaking bread."[1] Each term expresses a certain aspect of the sacrament.

Holy Communion is an act of sharing intimate fellowship. It is this kind of intimate union with God that we seek and are granted when we partake of the sacramental elements of Communion. Our Wesleyan tradition calls it "an outward sign of inward grace." It is a moment of symbolic union between the supplicant and God.

In the Gospels, the Lord's Supper provides an exquisite description of this sacrament. Jesus has arranged for the Passover meal to be celebrated. He is the host; it is the Lord's Supper. Jesus has "eagerly desired to eat this Passover" (Luke 22:15) with his disciples. He leads them in the ancient ritual of remembrance of the faithfulness of God during the Israelites' flight from Egypt. They remember their bondage and their freedom and express their gratitude in prayer and song. Jesus' blessing of the bread and wine at this supper transforms this already potent ritual.

This was a powerful moment in Christ's ministry. With the simple, everyday actions of eating and drinking, he creates a new covenant and proclaims our sins forgiven. "The celebration at the table marks, at the least, a deepening of the meaning of the everyday grace of God."[2] It is not enough that the first disciples share this meal with Christ. He commanded that we "do this in remembrance of [him]" (Luke 22:19b), and that all disciples continue this celebration. Every time we eat the bread and drink from the cup, we are to experience his love and grace anew. The sustenance provided in this ritual strengthens and encourages us on our faith journeys as did the manna provided for the Israelites during their Exodus.

His sacrifice and love offer us new opportunities for life. We are invited to the table by Jesus with all our blemishes and sins. We are served a meal rich in history, meaning, and love. This meal has been shared by Christ's disciples throughout the centuries. It is the source of our redemption and a reminder of God's presence in our hearts, minds, and bodies. "The bread and wine of Jesus' table is our path into the heart of the Holy and the Holy into our very bellies."[3] This moment of reconciliation between God and God's creation is repeated for our sake, for our remembrance. His sacrifice sets us free for a new relationship with God. "All this is from God, who reconciled us to himself through Christ, and has given us the ministry of reconciliation" (2 Corinthians 5:18).

The celebration of Communion is an act of thanksgiving. In fact, another term for Holy Communion is Eucharist. "*Eucharist* is made up of two Greek roots, *eu* meaning *good* or *well*, and *charis*, meaning *gift* or *grace*. These roots are also found in the traditional prayer that Jesus and his disciples repeated at Passover and other meals:

> *Blessed are you, O Lord our God, King of the Universe,*
> *Who brings forth bread from the earth.*
> *Blessed are you, O Lord our God, King of the Universe,*
> *Who creates the fruit of the vine.*"[4]

In the United Methodist celebration of Holy Communion, the consecration of the elements and the sharing of those elements are called The Great Thanksgiving.[5] Indeed, we are thankful for God's steadfast, reconciling love, for the gifts of life and food and all good things.

Our response to this wonderful gift is enthusiastic thanks. "As we commune, we express joyful thanks for God's mighty acts throughout history—for creation, covenant, redemption, sanctification."[6] Thanks is sung in praises, prayed in the heart, and lived out in our lives. Thanks fills our individual and collective hearts. In many ways this is a personal moment for each person at the table. We take in the bread and wine and our individual bodies are restored in the sacrament. But, however personal our relationship with Christ may be, the table is set and open to all. It is indeed an unusual circumstance to participate in Communion individually.

"Holy Communion is the communion of the church—the gathered community of the faithful, both local and universal. While deeply meaningful to the individuals participating, the sacrament is much more than a personal event. The first person pronouns throughout the ritual are consistently plural—*we, us, our*. . . . The sharing and bonding experienced at the Table exemplify the nature of the church and model the world as God would have it be."[7]

The community of faith shares together the gifts at the Lord's Table. "At the table we do get a sense of union with others. . . . Eating and drinking together creates community."[8] As we commune, we become aware of God's great love for humanity, the worth and the needs of other people, and are reminded of our responsibility to one another.

The gifts of grace and hope in Holy Communion require a human response. It requires the feelings, words, and actual acts of thanksgiving. We are compelled to express the compassion of Christ through acts of caring and kindness toward those we encounter in our daily lives.[9]

"The work of thanksgiving is that process of incorporation and transformation. . . .Generosity is born out of the work of thanksgiving. The circle of the gift is sustained. . . . The burden of obligation gives way to 'a lingering and generalized gratitude.' This is similar to the comfortable satiation and joy that accompanies a delicious meal shared with loved ones."[10]

We extend the blessings of the Communion table in our daily lives as we live in community. The celebration of the Eucharist empowers community as we reaffirm our commitment to the family of God. "We eat and drink both in acknowledgment of common loyalty and in anticipation of being strengthened for discipleship. It is the community that Christ formed and, in spite of the fact that we are individually members of it, the community is nonetheless primary."[11]

It is in community that we live out our covenant. It is in the faces of others that we see Christ. It is in our relationships with others that our acts of thanksgiving are lived out and passed on. It is in community that we are transformed and the Kingdom of God can be revealed.

It is at the table—the Communion table, the kitchen table, the dinner table—that community is formed. "Eating is a time for delighting not only in the food but also in each other. Eating together can heal old rifts, head off new ones, and build community."[12] Without eating together, a community splinters and decays.

A district superintendent in Pennsylvania was appointed to a district in crisis. There was no community, the pastors were disgruntled, and morale was low. His instructions were to rebuild morale.

First he met with the district pastors and he asked them this question: "When was the last time you ate in each other's homes?" The group responded that this had really not been done. One pastor commented that perhaps there had been a chat over coffee in a restaurant every once in a while. When the district superintendent stated that this should become a practice for them, there was resistance to the idea. As he left the meeting, he replied that he could do nothing about morale if they were not eating in each other's homes.

Hospitality in the Holy Land
by Joyce Wiggins, Memphis Conference

In March, 1998, I was a member of a Volunteers in Mission team to Bethlehem which was a combination medical and construction team. I was assigned to the Beit Sahour Medical Center to work with the nursing staff.

One morning I was invited to accompany the physician and nurses to the clinic in the Muslim community of Husan. Nurse Maha asked me to join her as she visited in the homes of the new mothers to assess their postpartum health. We visited several homes. I was invited to enter each home, remove my shoes, and sit. I was allowed to hold the infant while the nurse examined the mother. Then someone in the household would prepare Turkish coffee and pass around a big box of chocolate candies. When we left one home, the women would follow us to the next, where we had coffee and chocolate again. The last home was that of a poor, very young mother. There was only one chair which was given to me and the baby was quietly placed in my arms. Coffee for one (me) was prepared on a small brazier. Surrounded by smiling Muslim women who spoke no English, I, who did not speak their language, shared with them the commonalities of women everywhere, there in that bare room—age, number of children, and the joys and trials of motherhood.

I had never experienced such hospitality and love from a group who had little to give but themselves. It was a very humbling experience.

Several years later, when the district superintendent was moved to another appointment, the morale of the district was at an all-time high. The pastors felt appreciated and were working as a team. The community had been rebuilt. The reason for the renewed community was that they had eaten together—in each other's homes. They had become reacquainted. They had reestablished trust and found communion with one another.

It is impossible to have a community without eating together. "Eating seals the bonds of friendship as it expresses and generates intimacy with others."[13] It is no wonder that so much of our church life is found gathered around tables filled with food. The food draws us together and the fellowship keeps us together.

> As you cannot go to heaven alone,
> Food is to be shared.
> Food is heaven.
> As you share the sight of heavenly stars,
> So food is something which must be shared,
> Food is heaven,
> When food passes your throat,
> You accent heaven in your body.
> Food is heaven.
> Ah! Food is something that must be shared.[14]
> Kim Chi Ha

A teenage boy was recounting a discussion he had had with several of his friends. "I said that when people sit down and eat together, something happens; something more than just the food. Everyone else said, no, you just order pizza and eat it. What's so great about eating together?"[15] This teenage boy, raised in the church, had glimpsed the powerful bond that can be created around the sharing of a meal. It is great to eat together. The food tastes better and seems to satisfy differently when eaten in community.

The church community is built on snacks or pizza at youth fellowship, refreshments and teas with United Methodist Women, fish fries, and potluck suppers. These are all invitations into deeper relationship in the church family.

Each week hundreds of congregations move from the worship setting to the fellowship hall where tables are laden with sweet and savory treats, coffee and tea. Here visitors, guests, and members of the congregation gather together to exchange welcoming greetings and good wishes for the coming week. The children and the adults weave in and out, giving them a chance to grow comfortable in each other's presence. In my church, it is high energy—crowded and loud—but always friendly and welcoming. The community of faith is open to all and shares in that goodness.

To reinforce our faith commitment and our community, the church gathers around food. My favorite is the potluck supper or covered dish dinner (depending on what part of the country you are in). These meals are festive times. The food is always wonderful because it was prepared with the purpose of sharing. I look forward to the new tastes and combinations available at these gatherings. Expressing delight in a particular dish is satisfying for both the cook and the diner. Bringing dishes to share, sharing recipes, and enthusiastically indulging in the bounty found at such a community gathering are ways of sharing our love and respect for one another. I love the fact that we sit down together. Sitting means that we have time for one another. Everyday stories tumble out on the table to become moments of humor or sorrow shared. The results of a prayer chain are celebrated. Old and new friends are welcomed. We are bound together as a community of faith in the sharing of food and fellowship.

This fellowship finds another expression in the various church fund-raisers that feature food. Pancake breakfasts, fish fries, bake sales, and pork roasts raise money for mission or a new appliance for the kitchen or to send some kids to camp. Couldn't we just give donations quietly during worship? We certainly do that too. However, the fund-raisers featuring food also bring out the joy and companionship these efforts afford, making the food even more satisfying.

In my youth group, we enjoyed most cooking breakfast for the congregation on Easter morning. We helped lead the sunrise service and then raced to the kitchen. Mixing the batter for pancakes, frying the bacon, filling the syrup containers, making the coffee, were efforts of love and sharing. We laughed and talked and kidded around. Not one of us would have missed that opportunity. We were an important part of the community. Yes, it raised money for a work trip or scholarships for camp. But even without the fund-raising part I think we would have done it for the pure joy of being together and giving something back to the church—our community.

And the church came. We always had a full house for our breakfasts. People came in and out all morning. They came, not because it was the best breakfast around but to support and show solidarity with us. They had the chance to talk to old friends, have coffee with the pastor, and revel in the energy and enthusiasm stuffed inside each pancake. Just remembering our Easter breakfasts, my heart is full of love. I remain deeply connected to that part of my church family that nurtured and loved me in return.

This same devotion and commitment that comes from the "breaking of bread" is what the early church found vital. The early church recognized the benefit to the community of a regularly shared meal. "Day by day, as they spent much time together in the temple, they broke bread at home and ate their food with glad and generous hearts, praising God and having the goodwill of all the people. And day by day the Lord added to their number those who were being saved" (Acts 2:46-47).

From great distances, Paul, Peter, and other New Testament letter writers kept strong ties with the faith communities they had eaten with. The relationships forged as they shared food reinforced their faith in God. The loving, caring communities of early Christians allowed them to tolerate disease, oppression, uncertainty, and even disagreement among themselves. Again we find great benefit in combining the nourishment of the body with nourishment of the spirit in a community of believers.

Native Americans and the Communion Table
by Rev. Anita Phillips, Executive Director of the Native
American Comprehensive Plan
(a member of Cherokee Nation, Oklahoma)

There are some essential biblical concepts to consider when studying stories of Native Americans in this country. One of the metaphors we often use is that of the common (or Communion) table as a biblically-based notion of a "coming together place" for humanity. It is a place for sharing resources and finding ways of living with justice and in peace together. The common table arises from the many tables Jesus Christ shared with his marginalized brothers and sisters and with those who both agreed and disagreed with his message.

A further biblical concept that complements and even further refines the common table of humanity is the idea that there is more than one way of sharing that can take place around the common table. Gleaning is one biblical mechanism for sharing that has much to say to us in 2008 about what and how we share with others. In the story of Ruth gleaning in the fields of Boaz, an essential component of her gleaning is that she shared the very

---

same grain that Boaz was bringing to his own table. It was not a substandard grain, not a grain that fell from his table by accident, or was thrown away. It was the very same grain his family ate every day. The opposite of sharing through gleanings is sharing though "leavings." Leavings in this case means what is left from the table after those who "have," have had their fill. Leavings are the unwanted, less than satisfactory, garbage that is left over for the "have nots." I believe that sharing through gleanings and not through leavings is the Creator's call upon those of us at the common table of the world so loved by the Creator.

This has implications for all aspects of our humanitarian work in the world and our vision of a shared common table that welcomes all, including Native Americans. I believe that the vast majority of sharing with Native American peoples in the US, whether from government or church entities, throughout history, has been through leavings. One need only examine the geographical areas that Native peoples have been relegated to on reservations, as a result of treaties, to understand that these lands were the unwanted leavings after the desirable lands were seized by non-Native entities.

Today we are all offered the option of sharing through gleanings or leavings. I pray that we gather at the common table, willing to share what we would serve to our own families, willing to offer the same economic opportunities we seek for ourselves, to those who "have not," and fighting the temptation to share only substandard opportunities to Native Americans and other individuals, groups, and nations.

As noted earlier, Christian fellowship must extend beyond the church. I am a preacher's kid. For the Sunday midday meal (or dinner in our household), we were often joined by friends and members of the congregation. Whether it was in our house or someone else's, the camaraderie of the fellowship hour would spill over into the meals. Opening our homes to share a meal connotes a relationship beyond mere acquaintance in our society. It is an overt statement of camaraderie and a spirit of good fellowship.[16] Eating together creates intimacy and community.

Food is also a healer of community. As we live with one another conflicts arise. We do not always act with caring and kindness toward one another. When we find ourselves at odds with one another through ignorance, thoughtlessness, anger, or malice, we must remember the forgiveness offered to each of us at Christ's table.

Communion Bread
by Marilyn Zehring, Women's Division Director

Denise Larsen is a member of Centenary United Methodist Church in Beatrice, Nebraska. Centenary is a church of approximately 850 members. Denise has been making Communion bread for special services at Centenary since 1997. She has also made the Communion bread for district and conference United Methodist Women meetings.

Denise says, "I feel the Holy Spirit near me as I mix the bread by hand. It is truly a personal journey and a time of growth for me. Making the bread has had a big impact on how I look at the elements. It has become almost an obsession that Communion bread be broken. The spiritual power that I feel when the flat bread is held up and broken is hard to put in words. Seeing the jagged, torn edges of the bread and receiving a piece of the bread that has been torn is very moving and humbling, remembering that this is CHRIST'S BODY BROKEN FOR ME. Communion that does not have broken bread leaves me thirsting for something more. The broken bread definitely fills my spiritual hunger. It fills a place deep in my soul of being a participant in that Upper Room 2000 years ago."

Denise's Communion Bread Recipe

2½ cups whole wheat flour
1½ cups white flour
2 teaspoons salt
1½ teaspoons baking powder
2 teaspoons sugar
2 tablespoons butter
1½ cups milk
1 cup dark honey

Mix all ingredients by hand. (It is a sticky mess.) When well mixed, divide into 4 round pans that have been brushed with olive oil. Pat out. (You may have to use flour on your fingers.) Brush the tops with olive oil. Bake at 350° for 10 to 12 minutes. Each round will serve 50 to 75 people. The bread freezes well.

Forgiveness between individuals is difficult, whether you are the offender or the offended. Food, as with the bread and wine of the Eucharist, can often be the mediator in a conflict. Just as the Holy Spirit seeks to intervene, comfort, and change hearts and minds, food can be the means by which forgiveness is requested or given and community restored.

One such instance in my life began with the gift of my favorite breakfast muffin. It appeared magically on my desk one morning. I looked around at my colleague and dear friend with a question in my eyes. She slowly explained that the previous day she had been short and rude to me and she wanted to apologize. I had not even recognized the slight. I had simply chalked it off to a bad day and had moved on. But she had been hurt by her words to me. The gift of a favorite food gave her the opportunity to apologize. It gave me a chance to reaffirm our friendship. We shared the muffin, warmed by our friendship and the assurance of forgiveness.

Sharing food during a moment of forgiveness can be profoundly moving. It evokes the memory of bread and wine shared during Holy Communion, the forgiveness offered, and the redemption received at the table. It is precisely God's promise of forgiveness and renewed life that allows us to live with compassion and love of neighbor.[17]

Serbian Orthodox Christians in the former Yugoslavia have a Christmas morning tradition that joins the sharing of food with forgiveness. Special bread is prepared for Christmas morning breakfast. The family gathers for breakfast and begins with the Lord's Prayer. "Before breaking bread, it is customary for family members to reconcile their conflicts. They admit the wrongs they have done and forgive one another. Then everyone stands and together they take the big round bread in their hands, all breaking off a piece at the same time."[18] The bread and wine of the Communion table reach beyond the formal expression of the ritual in our lives when confession and acceptance are reenacted within the community of faith. Our hunger for sustenance beyond that of physical need is satisfied when we accept each other with the same grace that Christ accepts us.

Saying Grace

And for all the food we share—bringing us closer together as a family, as a community of faith, and sealing our commitment to one another—we thank God. A prayer of thanksgiving for the food God has provided is a logical expression of faith. It was considered such an important part of a faithful life that Deuteronomy instructs us to thank God when we eat (Deuteronomy 8:10).

When all eyes (and stomachs) are focused on the meal, a prayer at the beginning refocuses those gathered on our need for God. We use this time to remind ourselves of our interdependency with the larger family of God. We recognize the source of all our joy and strength. It is an act of worship.

Saying grace is gratitude. "Gratitude," writes John Mogabgab, "gathers us in that double helix of grace descending and praise ascending that forms the basic design of life with God." It is "the gesture of a heart opened to receive God"; it "refreshes our minds with the memory of God's gracious way."[19]

In such an "attitude of gratitude," grace is a free-flowing, all-encompassing expression of life and community.

> Between sewing and nutrition classes [in rural Honduras], we would quickly light a fire and make lunch. As we sat down to eat, [one of the women] would stop and look at the pile of tortillas we had patted out. Then with her eyes open to the world around her, she addressed God in a most intimate way.
>
> "God be with my children, may they always have enough food. Maribel's oldest child is sick; please lend your healing hand. Be with Marixa away in high school. May the people where she is staying treat her well and, God, bless her as she grows up. Please help Francis and Angela listen to their teachers and learn well today. . . ." She prayed in this way for each of her own children and for

many of the sewing students and people in her community. Then to close she said, "Gracious God, there are many hungry people, many children who cannot eat this lunch with us. God, please give them food to eat and bless us with this food. Thank you. Amen."

When [prayer] was finished, the tortillas were never as hot as they had been when they were set on the table, but meals with [these women] were truly blessed.[20]

In blessing the meal, we bless ourselves. The gratitude expressed reflects back on us. This reflection fills us with joy and strength. "The experience of saying grace is powerful because it communicates the theological meanings. . . . that connect the everyday, practical, holistic sense of lived experience with the transcendent source of the practice—Jesus."[21] In our prayer we find our place in the world.

The theology can seem complex but it can also be very simple. It can be so simple that saying grace is often the first instance in which children learn about God's deep and abiding love for them.

Grace is a wonderful learning tool for children. By saying grace, children learn the importance of God's presence at the table. As they pray, they connect God and the food on the table. The food that sustains our bodies is provided by God. God loves us and wants us to live healthy and happy lives. For God's love and the food we say a prayer of thanks and praise.

In our home, we hold hands around the table. The circle formed by our hands illustrates the support and trust that we have in one another. The unity expressed this way is the basis of the community of faith that exists throughout the world. We are connected one to another through the love of Christ.

Graces differ from family to family, from denomination to denomination, and from faith expression to faith expression. They are usually short, memorized verses, but they can also be spontaneous, short prayers of thanks.

Many of the traditional graces used in the US today may be traced to *The Book of Common Prayer*. They succinctly thank God for our sustenance—spiritual and physical. These prayers of thanksgiving weave together the recognition of the fact that food for the body and food for the soul are inexorably linked together and to the larger community of God's family.

Familiar Graces

Thank you, Lord, for this food which is set before us.
May we use it to nourish our bodies, as you nourish our souls.
Make us ever more mindful of the needs of others.
Through Christ Our Lord, Amen.

Dear Lord, thank you for this food.
Bless the hands that prepared it.
Bless it to our use and us to your service,
And make us ever mindful of the needs of others.
Through Christ our Lord we pray. Amen.

God is great!
God is good!
Let us thank God
For our food. Amen.

"Johnny Appleseed Grace"
Oh, the Lord's been good to us,

And so we thank the Lord,
For giving us the things we need,
The sun and the rain and the appleseed.

Come, Lord Jesus
Be our guest
And let these gifts
To us be blest!

Blessed be God
Who is our bread!
Let all the world
Be clothed and fed!

When we offer our thanks, we invite Christ into our midst. The Wesleyan grace, whether recited or sung, is a traditional prayer often used by United Methodists. Its first line is very clearly an invitation, an appeal to God to be with us now and always.

"Be present at our table, Lord;
be here and everywhere adored;
thy creatures bless, and grant that we
may feast in paradise with thee."[22]

This grace invites Christ to the table as a member of the family, as Jesus invites us to the Lord's Supper. The intimacy of this invitation bespeaks the intimacy of the Communion rite expressed in everyday life.

It is this very intimacy that sometimes stops us cold when a grace is suggested in a public setting. We may feel that it is something private, something we do at home, or not appropriate in the eyes of our fellow diners. "For many of us, saying grace at the table feels awkward, trite, or even annoying. This is not because giving thanks for the food is a stupid idea. More likely, it is because we have never devoted attention to making this ritual all it can be."[23]

Perhaps we should take a lesson from the children. My nieces and nephews are the first to insist that we say grace wherever we are—around a campfire or a kitchen table. It could be a tailgate party or a doll's tea party and we would still say grace. I have come to appreciate their need for the consistent application of gratitude. Their simple theology with its consistency trumps the inconsistent use of my multifaceted theology.

Regardless of where we eat, we should take a moment to recall the blessings of the table set in front of us. For many people, public grace is embarrassing and uncomfortable. Here are some ways people have found to bless their food in public. L. Shannon Jung is a self-described "militant grace-sayer in public restaurants."[24] We aren't all comfortable with that. I have been with friends and colleagues who look each other directly in the eye and very conversationally give thanks for the gifts before us. I have taken a silent moment with my head bowed when traveling alone.

Saying grace is important. It is so easy to become inured to being fed on command. In the US it is a common occurrence to eat out. When food is ordered and placed in front of us, we can forget where it came from. The plate has appeared in front of us without any effort on our part. Before we begin to believe that the food came to us without effort, say grace. Or before we begin to believe that the food we eat is our right, say grace. Or before we begin to believe that we deserve this bounty, say grace.

Say thank you for the sun and the rain that created the food. Express your gratitude for the people who picked, produced, and packaged the food. Appreciate the preparers, cooks, and wait staff for your meal. But, most of all, be grateful for the source of all good things. God is "the Divine Chef."

When we take the time to truly focus our thoughts on God and God's blessings, we experience the filling of our spirits with spiritual bounty. We realize, in our expressions of thanksgiving, that it is God and the people around us that satisfy our deeper hunger. "We find that in giving thanks we receive the gift of gratitude. Thanks to God for his goodness, for the gift of Jesus and our life in him, is the key to joy."[25]

CHAPTER 2

Image of God

So God created humankind in his image,
in the image of God he created them;
male and female he created them (Genesis 1:27).

Or do you not know that your body is a temple
of the Holy Spirit within you, which you have
from God, and that you are not your own? (1 Corinthians 6:19).

What do you see when you look in the mirror? Do you see beauty or mediocrity? Are you pleased with your image or do you wish for improvement? If this is all you see, look a little harder. When you look in the mirror, you see a portion of what God looks like. You are created in the image of God. You are a beloved child of God, a beautiful creation of God.

As Christians filled with the Holy Spirit, we hold within us the companion and comforter promised by God. God does not live in the church buildings we have created. God dwells within each of us. We are filled with God's presence, the Holy Spirit. Each of us is a unique temple, a holy place, and we are the trustees.

The dwelling place of God's spirit—our body—is sacred and requires care to keep it strong and solid. It should be cared for as attentively and lovingly as we would care for Jesus himself. Our bodies are built and strengthened by the food God provides for us, our spirits by God's love.

This reality often gets neglected as we respond to the day-to-day necessities of life. We see only the image of ourselves when we gaze into the mirror. It is too easy to forget that in that gaze we glimpse God.

Take a moment and look at yourself. Look at God's beautiful creation. Recognize the Spirit that lives within you.

It is difficult to admit to ourselves that we do see God in our image. If we really take in that truth, it can be overwhelming. Each of us is a reflection of God through God's love and grace. When we accept Christ into our lives, we recognize the Christ within us. We strive to nurture and nourish our faith without acknowledging that the way in which we feed ourselves is very much a part of our faith commitment. Everything we have comes from God, every morsel we eat is God's creation.

We ignore the way we eat food at the risk of breaking Christ's commands.

> "Teacher, which commandment in the law is the greatest?" [Jesus] said to him, "You shall love the Lord your God with all your heart, and with all your soul, and with all your mind." This is the greatest and first commandment. And a second is like it: "You shall love your neighbor as yourself" (Matthew 22:36-38).

The insight Jesus shares with this scripture is striking. "...Jesus summarized the law by elevating love for neighbor to a place right beside love for God....The two are not the same, but they cannot be separated, either."[1] Our love for God is inextricably linked with our love for others and our love for ourselves. Love our neighbors as ourselves. This scripture does more than recognize the call to treat our neighbors well. We are not instructed to love our neighbor better than ourselves or instead of ourselves. No. We are to care for ourselves **as much as—the same as**—our family and our neighbors. How well do we live out this scripture? Is your love for yourself separate from your love for God? Do you see your self-esteem and self-respect as an important part of the way you cherish God's presence in your life?

If we are truly going to live out these two commandments as Jesus has stated them, we have to decide where we fall in our list of priorities. We are not last on the list. God commands that we care for ourselves with the same attention and love as we care for others. How we care for ourselves is as important to God as caring for others. Our bodies are sacred[2] and what we do with our bodies is important.

How we treat our bodies, how and what we feed our bodies, and how healthy we keep our bodies is important because our bodies are sacred. Here is an essential point where food and faith intersect.

There are two things that keep us from daily recognizing how the food we eat fundamentally affects our relationship with God—the busyness of our lives and the unconscious manner in which we feed ourselves.

Busyness and Food

Today, more than ever before, Americans are busy. We are "busy with work, errands, e-mail, driving, and shopping . . . the average American spends 72 minutes daily driving, a typical business executive loses 68 hours a year on hold on the telephone."[3] Add to this list, sports, music, homework, karate, or any other activity that your children or grandchildren may be involved in and you have a very busy American family. Single people are not immune. They have their own activities that congest their schedules.

This kind of schedule often leads people to make food choices based on expediency and convenience. Fast food is regularly the meal for the family on-the-go. Drive-through service allows food to be passed through the car in handy portions and it is eaten buckled-in and moving. Pickles and potatoes are the vegetables and processed frozen meat the entrée. There is opportunity for conversation. We see each other's faces in the rear view mirror. One of the kids even says, "Thanks, mom." A nod to quality family time, no hungry bellies, and we weren't late. That is a successful day. Tomorrow it starts all over again.

Pickle Hospitality
by Joyce Wiggins, Memphis Conference

I have a friend who is now 83 years old. She has discovered a way to make gift giving easier, more economical and tasty. She has a recipe for sweet pickles created from adding sugar and pickling spices to a gallon jar of dill pickle slices. Friends supply the recycled jars. Her "special son" is responsible for washing the jars and tightening the lids. Starting in January and working at her leisure, she creates 4 to 6 gallons of sweet pickles each year. She gives them to friends at Christmas, as hostess and birthday gifts, and to her doctors and staff. Everyone loves the pickles but, even more, they love her and her spirit of hospitality.

Did you taste the food that you ate? Did you recognize that the food did more than refuel you? Did you thank God for nourishment that is available to you only because of God's creation? Did the meal remind you of your reliance on God for all things? Did it even occur to you to ask yourself any of these questions? If not, you are not alone.

Americans are known for their busyness— "hurried, running from one thing to the next, unable to relax and enjoy themselves."[4]

People complain about their busy schedules with a mixture of exasperation and pride. Busyness is the direct result of the center point of our culture—achievement. "In America, the preferred worldview is that 'doing' is most sensible since it leads to achievement."[5]

Food Rationing in Cuba—God Always Provides
by Nelida Mora-Morales, Women's Division Director
(2000-2008)
Iglesia Cristiana Juan Wesley, Metodista Unida
Miami, Florida

I had a personal experience in Cuba. When Castro's revolution took over the country, almost every food item was rationed—even those produced in the country. We had to live by faith, waiting each day for whatever was coming to the store and what we were eligible to buy. It did not matter if we had the money. You could only buy what you were eligible to buy. People could try to buy food in the black market and take the risk of going to jail if caught. Government spies were everywhere and always ready to denounce you.

Since all private land was expropriated from the owners, they had to grow what the government asked them to grow. Many of them hid small gardens to grow crops for their own use and we were able to buy some things in hiding. God provided always.

The scriptural passage about Jesus feeding the thousands (found not only in John but in all the Gospels), was very relevant for me. I also experienced the multiplication of whatever little food the church in Cuba had to feed delegates at meetings and gatherings. It was incredible how people brought whatever they could, sometimes their own ration of food, and how the thousands

---

were fed. These days it has been easier to find ways to buy food with the help of outside resources and hard currency. In many ways, we see the Lord providing for the needs of his people.

The emphasis on "doing" in our culture means that it is the end result of the activity that is valued. It is not the food that is important, it is the refueling. By refueling, we treat our bodies like machines that have specific tasks to perform instead of bodies with purpose and spirit. Refueling is done quickly, like a pit crew in a race. Service the machine as quickly as possible, and get it back on the road. This is particularly noticeable in the speed at which we eat.

Most Americans eat too fast. In our efforts to refuel, we deny ourselves pleasure and nutrition. We also eat too much in the process. We would do well to remember an African proverb, "Don't take another mouthful before you have swallowed what is in your mouth."[6] Our penchant for eating quickly results in "tak[ing] in too many calories before [we] realize [we've] eaten enough. It takes approximately 20 minutes from the time you start eating for your brain to send out signals of fullness. Leisurely eating allows ample time to trigger the signal from your brain that you are full. And feeling full translates into eating less."[7]

The impact of our busy lives on our eating habits stands juxtaposed to the deep spiritual nature of our faith. Our relationship with God is to be our primary goal. It is so easy for our relationship with God to be obscured in our daily lives. How are we to bring God back into sharp focus? There are many ways for this to happen, many methods to employ to remind ourselves of the importance of God in our lives.

It is both amusing and sad that we must be reminded to acknowledge our reliance on God on a daily basis. Wherever we look we see the wonder of God's creation. Everything that we eat demonstrates the gifts of God's love. Nevertheless, we seem to need a way to bring our attention back to God.

Eating food is an ancient way to celebrate our relationship with God, consecrated by Jesus as the ultimate memory device. "Do this in remembrance of me." The act of Communion is not restricted to the small symbols of bread and wine ritually received in church. Each act of eating should serve as a reminder of God's presence in our lives.

Instead, eating has become an activity of refueling to support our busy schedules like filling the gas tank on the car. It is a necessary activity. In our busy lives, it takes some conscious refocusing to make eating a moment of praise, thanks, and recommitment to our Christian faith.

In the act of eating, experience the blessing that food is. Recognize that the nutrition your body will draw from the food represents the nourishment your spirit enjoys through Christ. When we add a prayer of thanksgiving and praise, we refocus, even momentarily, on the fact that our relationship with God is the center point of our lives as Christians.

For one week, try to refocus your attention to the act of eating and how it represents our reliance on God. I think you will find that your spirit is nurtured along with your body. What difference does it make in your life to have your spirit fed to sustain you through your busy schedule?

Being busy isn't always about "doing." For many people the act of staying busy is a way to disconnect from self and others. Staying busy can keep us from being fully present. Sharyn Rose, a Massachusetts therapist, says being busy can lead "to a complete disconnection with our relationships with others and with ourselves and with society in general."[8]

Eating on the run to meet a busy schedule adds to the

disconnection Ms. Rose talks about. Is your schedule allowing you to put distance between you and your family, your friends, God? It is human nature to fail to see what we are avoiding. It is harder to admit that sometimes we neglect the most important parts of our lives.

Take some time at each meal to look deeply at each person gathered for the meal. Try to recognize the reflection of God that they represent. Deliberately calm the whirling of your mind and listen to the conversation. Try to contribute personal comments. Keep your talk about work minimal. And thank God silently or audibly for the richness of your life.

Unconscious Eating

The refueling aspect of consuming food can be called unconscious eating. However, unconscious eating is much more complicated for many Americans. Unconscious eating is about how we choose what and where to eat, with whom we eat, and when we eat. When we become actively conscious about how and why we eat, we can make better choices and gain the added benefit of spiritual sustenance.

What Do We Eat

Making food choices is difficult. Shopping takes time and planning, although we often approach shopping with little time and no real planning. We are told that we should make healthy choices, but every day new information is being released on how best to stay healthy. And tomorrow it could all change again. Fortunately, we are given guidelines which can help us in making good choices.

The US Department of Agriculture has updated the food pyramid which had been a guide for healthy meal choices and a healthy lifestyle for more than two generations. Today the food pyramid is a rainbow of vertical stripes with stair steps up the left side. It speaks to the need to include grains, vegetables, fruits, milk, beans, and meat in proper amounts to have a healthy diet. The food pyramid not only gives guidance on food choices, it also recommends exercise. The rainbow is broader at the bottom than at the top, indicating that one size *doesn't* fit all. It encourages personalization based on age, gender, and physical activity level. These guidelines together with these God-given foods make a nutritional diet possible.

However, our choices are often made based on our busy schedules. Many of us try to choose healthy foods—foods that will give our bodies the greatest nutrition. But most of the time convenience and ease of preparation make the final decisions. Fresh food is healthy but requires preparation. Instead we rely on canned, frozen, and processed foods for meals. (Ninety percent of the average American's food budget is spent on processed food.)[9] We read the labels but labels can be hard to decipher.[10] Product marketing says something is healthy, so we choose that. We have busy lives. It is often easier to take advertising at face value than to take the time to do some critical evaluation of our own.

This is a part of unconscious eating. Making food decisions based on convenience and health benefits leaves out a crucial component. Would the decisions we make be more conscious if we kept God and the sustenance we will derive from our choices clearly in our mind while shopping? Can we change the decision-making priorities we use when shopping? Can we give healthy choices priority over convenience and ease? If we do not have time to feed our bodies in healthy and satisfying ways, are we taking the time to feed our spirits?

The unconscious nature of our food choices is not the only unconscious part of our eating. We eat too much. We know that when we eat to refuel we eat too quickly and make food choices based on convenience. And isn't it convenient to say "supersize it!"?

If we replay the drive-through meal at the beginning of this chapter, it is easy to hear the words "supersize it!" expanding the portions being passed through the car. In general, a regular order from any fast food establishment will satisfy the appetite of most people. The problem is that eating on the run means that we eat the meal that we have chosen so quickly that we do not give our bodies enough time to recognize "the feeling of satisfaction or fullness, the lack of desire to eat more, the need to rest while the food digests, perhaps a bit of thirst."[11] So we "supersize it" to make sure that we are actually full.

Without saying the words, we "supersize" our meals in other ways. We help ourselves to second and third helpings. One serving is sufficient to assuage our appetite in most instances. Taking a second or third helping is about taste, comfort, or even generosity.

My husband's mother showed her love and affection through her cooking during her life. To her, the quantity her family and guests ate was in direct proportion to how much they loved and appreciated her. A favorite family story aptly illustrates her generosity and its reflection on her.

While in college, my husband had invited a friend, Tom, to dinner one evening. After everyone had had their first helping, his mother invited Tom to have another helping of roast beef. He respectfully declined. Again she urged him to have more meat, and again he declined. So she finally turned to my husband and said, "Son, put some roast beef on Tom's plate." How could he refuse? Tom dutifully ate the extra helping of meat.

How many times have I heard, "There is plenty left. Go back for seconds." "Would someone please finish this up? There is not enough for leftovers and I don't want to throw it out." I have heard something like this at nearly every family gathering, church supper, and community event throughout my life. It is meant in a spirit of generosity. But it encourages bad habits and overeating. Our bodies do not use the extra food efficiently when we overeat. The calories and nutrition in the extra helping does not increase our nourishment and can actually be harmful to our health. There are very few people in America today who are not aware of this fact.

Hospitality is a central point where food and faith converge. We explore this at length in chapter three. However, as we provide hospitality it is important to keep in mind that overfeeding is not the same thing as generosity. Practicing the generosity of enough runs counter to our culture but it is worth considering when we are hosting others. Can we make up for small quantities of food in other ways? Plan for longer meals. Encourage animated, soulful conversation. Make more courses and serve them at intervals to insure that everyone can recognize the feeling of fullness and satisfaction. At such occasions, Christ's presence is present in abundance. "For where two or three are gathered in my name, I am there among them" (Matthew 18:20). Can the joy and camaraderie experienced in the meal add to the satisfaction?

Where Do We Eat?

I have a confession to make. I have a terrible habit. I eat lunch at my desk nearly every day. I have a desk full of things to do and I convince myself that I can leave at 4:30 p.m. instead of 5:00 p.m. by doing this, although I don't always leave by 4:30 p.m. My friends come by and say, "Come to lunch." Sometimes I take them up on it; most times I don't.

I know that eating at my desk is bad for me. It is as bad for me as eating in front of the television set. When I eat at my desk, I am unconsciously eating. I don't think about the nutrition I am getting from my food. Sometimes I'm not even aware of what I am eating, let alone how it tastes, and I love the way food tastes! It is one of my favorite pleasures. And I often don't say a word of grace or reflect on God's blessings evident in my meal. [I have made a commitment to overcome my bad habit. I am consciously working to revise my work eating patterns in more positive ways.]

I am not alone in my sorry choice of eating place. Many single people eat while standing up—often in front of the sink to avoid washing dishes. "About 40 percent of Americans always or often watch television while eating dinner, according to the National Institute of Media and the Family."[12] "Nineteen percent of meals [and snacks in the US] are eaten in the car."[13]

When we eat by ourselves and/or eat while engaged in other activities, we are not receiving the full benefit food has to offer. Again we are only refueling. Eating with friends and family enhances the food with the flavor of companionship, draws out the richness of our interdependency, and celebrates the blessings God gives to our bodies and our spirits.

With Whom Do We Eat?

Too often we eat alone, or in front of the TV, or in the car. A meal is supposed to be more than getting our minimum daily requirement. As we learned in chapter one, a meal is at its best when it takes place as part of community and is shared. It should be a time to remember our connections to God and each other.

The value of the ancient tradition of sharing meals in community can today be proven by science. When we eat at table with others our bodies benefit. "Contrast a family-around-the-table meal at home to a meal at home with the television. The more often that children eat in front of the television, the more likely they are to get more of their calories from fatty meats, pizza, salty snacks, and soda, and the less likely they are to get them from fruits and vegetables. Children in high-television-meal families also average twice as much caffeine consumption as do their peers."[14]

These statistics are useful as we review our eating habits. But science only puts numbers and values to something we have known all along—eating is a fuller, more satisfying experience when we eat with others.

When possible, make a point of seeking out meal companions. Refer to the chapter on hospitality and actively reach out to others to enrich your meal. Schedule your meals so that they allow you to eat with family and friends.

When I eat alone at my desk, I am separated from my friends and colleagues. Working through lunch, I do not take advantage of some of the benefits I could extract from my solo eating experience. I am refueling, not celebrating the gifts God has so generously bestowed.

When and How Do We Eat?

When you do eat alone, take full advantage of it. In fact, you are not eating alone. God is always present and a willing meal companion. Engage in conversation with God. Be thankful and remember that the "breaking of bread" recalls God's gift of Christ.

You defy American culture if you eat only at breakfast, lunch, and dinner. Most Americans eat whenever their appetite is active. We snack. We snack for a brief spurt of energy between meals, or purely for the gratification of the taste (and more, as we shall see). Sometimes it is hard to determine which.

Appetite does not always indicate hunger. It can also be an urge to satisfy a perceived need. When appetite is not hunger, we overeat.

"Overeating is not eating. Eating is a natural way of giving sustenance to our bodies. Smartly, we're designed to enjoy food so that we ensure our own survival but stop when we've had enough so we don't make our bodies unwell."[15] God has created us in such a way that our bodies trigger a feeling of fullness or satisfaction when we have eaten enough. When we continue to eat, ignoring our bodies' signals, we are eating unconsciously.

Many people enjoy the taste of food and will ignore the feeling of fullness in favor of taste. One person wondered, "What if the taste of food didn't exist? … [then] we wouldn't need to eat unhealthy tasty foods."[16] This is a wonderful fantasy but God created us to delight in the food given to sustain us. It is up to each of us to choose to listen to our bodies or push beyond our limits. When we eat for taste there are usually two other unrecognized factors present. We are not eating at mealtime, and the taste is a substitute for another unmet need.

Food can "be a distraction. If you're worried about an upcoming event or rethinking an earlier conflict, eating comfort foods may distract you. But the distraction is only temporary. While you're eating, your thoughts focus on the pleasant taste of your comfort food. Unfortunately, when you're done overeating, your attention returns to your worries."[17]

A colleague said to me in frustration and concern, "My mother is a nurse. She knows all the health risks she faces by being overweight. But she is still overweight." Recent studies show that over 65 percent of us fall into the same category. It is difficult to move past our unconscious eating. Dieting is not the answer. It is the short-term solution for deep-seated behavior.

When we turn to food to distract us from fear, worry, or anger, what do we really want? Are we looking for comfort and consolation? Are we feeling overwhelmed and lonely? If we can recognize that our desire or craving for food is not prompted by hunger, we have an opportunity to move past our unconscious eating into a level of self-awareness that could help change our behavior. "Look at how you are feeling, what state you are in, and how familiar this feeling is. Without judgment, instead with curiosity and respect, look at the trigger of the craving."[18] Are you longing for a friend, a hug, a lover, a reward, a mother? Could it be that you are craving appreciation, recognition, approval, respect? Are your yearnings a protection against the fear of scarcity, attention, relationships? Then you are not looking for the nourishment that is found in food. Food is not your friend or a gold medal. Food is a gift from God that should bring you closer to God. When food is not nourishment for your body, it cannot be nourishment for your spirit.

Is the comfort that food provides a substitute for the comfort God can give? Are we confusing the intricate relationship between God and food and focused on the gift instead of the source? Is Christ able to provide in full what the food can only provide in part?

These are questions which may begin a change in the way we think about food but will not get to the root of everyone's issues around overeating. More than six out of ten adult Americans weigh too much according to the National Institutes of Health.[19] Americans are overwhelmed by their bounty. The bounty that most of us take for granted, the choices that we have, and our busy schedules are all relatively new phenomena. Our bounty has created concepts like overeating, eating healthy, and healthy weight. In the ancient world, there was no long-term bounty. You spent your day struggling to feed yourself and your family. Before agriculture was developed (around 10,000 BCE), the largest part of every person's day was spent hunting and gathering wild food. You were either healthy or not. And there was no question about the relationship between God and food. After the domestication of food plants and animals (agriculture), humans were able to distribute the workload throughout communities, villages, towns, and even city-states. This division of labor and the ability to build up limited surpluses of food allowed much of the population to engage in non-farming activities. However, all activities required energy and exercise, and food supplies could not always be relied upon. During this time your access to food was directly related to where you were on the scale of wealth or poverty. If people could indulge themselves to the point of being overweight, they were presumed wealthy. Being underweight, in general, meant limited access to food, which was associated with poverty. This reality began to change in the 19th century with the advent of industrialization.[20]

Food and Hospitality
By Nelida Mora-Morales, Women's Division Director
(2000-2008)
Iglesia Cristiana Juan Wesley, Metodista Unida
Miami, Florida

In our church, there are people from many countries: Cuba, Puerto Rico, Colombia, Nicaragua, Costa Rica, Dominican Republic, Venezuela, and probably others that I do not know; but hospitality is a common denominator. Each Sunday a team prepares lunch with different choices for the small congregation. It is an opportunity to share together like in the Upper Room. Those able to donate the food or give an offering for the expenses of the food to help raise extra funds do so, but we share the food with all, no matter what their situation may be. We also keep a small food bank to help needy families.

I praise God for all the blessings and the opportunities we have to be in mission through food and hospitality.

Our postindustrialized society expects abundant and stable supplies of food. Most Americans have no direct relationship with actual food production. Ask any suburban or city kid where food comes from and you will hear, "the grocery store!" Although most of us know where food comes from, we would be hard-pressed to produce it ourselves. This creates a kind of magical thinking that food is always accessible or that food is eternal.

Americans have a divided understanding of food. Our instincts tell us that food is temporary. Our daily lives tell us food is eternal and without limit.

Since the beginning, humans have lived in a cycle of feast and famine. Today that cycle is still the reality for many throughout the world. "In the language of the Iteso people of Eastern Uganda, as in many African languages, each month of the year is given a descriptive name. August—the month after the millet harvest is 'the month of the big stomach' but, in poignant contrast, the pre-harvest month of May, when the granaries are empty, is 'the month when the children wait for food.'"[21]

Recently, I was told about a toddler who had been adopted from a poor country by an American family. After they had had her home with them for a few days, they became concerned that her cheeks had become puffy. One night the mother examined the sleeping child to find a significant stash of uneaten food in her cheeks. Just like a chipmunk, the child was storing food in her cheeks against the possibility of scarcity. The child had not yet learned to trust that food would be ample and available in her new home. It took the child well over a year before she felt secure enough to discontinue this practice.

How much hunger did it take for an 18-month-old child to learn to hoard food? She had experienced continuous food shortage. It wasn't that the orphanage had the food and wasn't sharing it. The entire country was experiencing food scarcity. Scarcity is the primary reason that humans over the centuries have faced hunger. And like this young girl, humanity remembers that shortages are always possible.

Our instinct tells us that food is scarce and valuable. Our daily lives tell us that food is cheap and available. This reality sets up a contradiction in many peoples' minds. We should eat food while it is plentiful in preparation for the scarcity to come.

For many Americans food scarcity doesn't come but other scarcities do appear. Are the scarcities that we face those of love, self-esteem, joy? Somewhere deep within, does it seem that all scarcity should be satiated by food? When these links exist, they are hidden deep within our hearts and minds. They are not easily identified, revealed, or revised. They are our food issues, our food attitudes that blind and bind us.

God can provide strength and comfort to us as we work through our issues with food but we must do the work to make and maintain the changes to our food attitudes. People have struggled with many problems that have separated them from God throughout history. In Lamentations, the author is in deep distress, convinced that God is the cause of his suffering. But he finally comes to a place where the falseness of this sentiment is revealed.

> The steadfast love of the Lord never ceases, his
> mercies never come to an end; they are new every
> morning; great is your faithfulness. "The Lord is
> my portion," says my soul, "therefore I will hope
> in him" (Lamentations 3:22-24).

Finally the way to address his struggle comes to him, "Let us test and examine our ways, and return to the Lord" (Lamentations 3:40).

We have been blessed with unconditional love and grace and free will. Drawing on these blessings, we need to take on the struggle to uncover the deep-seated roots of our food issues. No one can do it for us. Not even God.

Our secular world addresses this reality in another way. It is called a mindset. People who are overweight or "obese have a poor relationship with themselves and food. The poor relationship with self exists in their not being aware of what the food … symbolizes to them. Just like the person who is obsessed with a lover or alcohol; they're all addictions that are symbols of inner conflict in beliefs about self and food. First, one has to recognize the inner emptiness the food is trying to fill and begin to take actions that start to satisfy that hunger without the food. Examine your beliefs about yourself and food. Secondly, get in the habit of focusing the mind on pleasures other than food. Food is not the problem. It's the relationship one has with it."[22]

If a person has a relationship with food that overshadows his/her relationship with God, changing the focus from food to God is a good first step. Engage in deep conversation with God to determine what food means to you. This conversation cannot be had in 15 minutes. Our relationship with food that overtakes our minds and hearts did not happen in 15 minutes. God is always ready to listen and bolster us in our efforts. A combination of self-reflection, prayer, and counseling can work together to heal one's relationship with food. It is God's greatest desire to help us reach our highest potential. God will not leave us comfortless.

It is not a struggle to be taken lightly. "People who have a poor relationship with food often suffer from tunnel vision. They tend to think a lot about food, in very imaginative ways. The thinking is habitual and repetitive without examination. Food has a very high ranking on their priority list."[23]

Food may guide our choices for activity, "I walked three blocks today! I deserve a cookie." Food sets our schedule for the day. Our days are split into segments divided by meals. Food directs our thoughts. A very popular television personality "whose battles with weight are well documented, thinks a lot about food. She has food that goes along with every activity. This is the same problem many people have. Too much focus on food."[24] If we find food the focus of our lives, how can we possibly adjust our focus to the betterment of our health and our relationship with God? Some people have found that they have other activities, other passions in their lives. "If you are doing things that you enjoy and can lose yourself in, your focus is on your activity and not what's good to eat."[25]

The habitual and repetitive thinking about food is not reserved for those who are overweight and obese. People with other eating disorders also obsess about food but in different ways. Between 5 to 10 percent of girls and women (i.e., 5-10 million people) and 1 million boys and men suffer from eating disorders, including anorexia, bulimia, binge eating disorder, or other associated dietary conditions.[26]

The relationship between people struggling with these disorders and food is most often one of power. They need strict control over their bodies. Young people, particularly young girls, find that controlling food intake makes them feel more sure of themselves and less vulnerable. Eating disorders seem to help them cope with the overwhelming feelings of adolescence. Many are using their control of food as a coping mechanism to protect themselves from physical, emotional, or sexual abuse, or other trauma. Insecurity and low self-esteem drive some people to put all their energy into how they look.[27]

The control that those with eating disorders inflict upon their bodies is frightening. We want a reason, a change, a cure. In reality, these disorders fall more into the categories of alcoholism and depression. All of these diseases are genetic predispositions that are activated by an unknown environmental trigger. No cure is possible but recovery can lead to a life of joy and triumph. The relationship between eating disorders and alcoholism is not only in the possible genesis of the disease. It is also in the most successful road to recovery—complete reliance on God.

> Humble yourselves before the Lord, and he will exalt you (James 4:10).

In *Over It – A Teen's Guide to Getting Beyond Obsessions with Food and Weight*, the authors put great emphasis on the nurturing of the spiritual self. "When we are caught up in our own world of struggling with food and weight, we forget that we are much more than our eating disorder. We forget that we are much more than our weight, what we just ate, our grades, or our friends. We forget that each and every one of us came from the same source of creation. We were all born with divine spirit. When we start to accept this, just as we accept our bodies and our feelings, we can stop fighting with ourselves and start enjoying ourselves."[28]

The food can blind us to the source of all things. Food becomes distorted in our minds as it beckons us with the empty promise of comfort and love. Or food is only recognized as the enemy that bars the way to joy and contentment. When this happens, only God has the strength to guide us back to recovery and a healthy understanding of its benefits.

The most successful approach to overcoming these kinds of distortion of mind and battles of spirit has been the Twelve-Step program, pioneered by the founders of Alcoholics Anonymous. These twelve steps have been successfully used, revised, and adapted for many different struggles of mind and spirit because of their utter reliance on God.

Our busy lives sometimes blur the glimpses of God available to us every day. Our image in a mirror, the warm sunshine, our families and friends, the food at our meals—these are all glimpses of God should we take the opportunity to recognize them. God offers us the opportunity to fill us with the richness and satisfaction of God's bounty. That bounty is both found in the harvest of grains, vegetables, fruits, fish, fowl, and other meats and as we recognize the nourishment of our bodies we feed our spirits on God's grace and abundant love.

The deep need of our souls for the reviving refreshment of God's grace is endless. The food we eat is the most visible manifestation of that need. Christ has blessed the meal as a reminder of his presence—an ever-present source of nourishment and strength.

CHAPTER 3

Hospitality – Sharing God's Bounty

S easoned travelers, my colleague and I were accustomed to negotiating our way through all types of obstacles, delays, and circumstances all over the world. On this particular trip, we were traveling by train on our way to southwest Hungary to visit a refugee camp. Neither of us spoke or understood Hungarian at all. About two hours into our four-hour train ride, the conductor came by our cabin and began speaking and gesticulating wildly. He broke off his rant and left us to wonder exactly what he might be trying to communicate. Seconds later the train stopped in the middle of the beautiful Hungarian countryside. It took some effort, but we finally began to understand that we had missed our transfer stop. We were now headed in the wrong direction.

The disturbance had, quite understandably, caught the attention of our fellow travelers. After a short time we found we could communicate on a rudimentary level with a family of women—a high school-age daughter, her mother, and grandmother. They described the journey before us. We needed to get off the train at another stop, take a bus to a town about 10 miles from our ultimate destination, and then call our contacts to come pick us up. It was daunting but what other option did we have? The train rumbled back into motion.

Later, in an attempt at communication, I handed the daughter my business card, which had the United Methodist cross and flame on it. Suddenly everything changed. The women instructed us to travel with them. We passed the stop where we were supposed to catch the bus and traveled further along the line.

We left the train with the women. A young man met them and was surprised to find that suddenly he had two more women in his care. After a brief walk, we entered a modest home and met the father and grandfather of the family. Momentarily befuddled, they welcomed us. We were led into their kitchen and served a light meal of scrambled eggs and pickles with a tube of paprika and a traditional beverage. This food strengthened our bodies and buoyed our spirits.

To our surprise, the grandmother arrived with a car (communally used by the town). She and her granddaughter loaded us into the car and drove us nearly two hours to our hotel in southwest Hungary. We spent a great deal of time persuading them to take even the smallest amount of money for gas. Only when it was explained as a gift would they accept it.

I now know only one word in Hungarian—köszönöm! (COO-ze-nam) or "thank you." And when I use that word, it is with reverence and wonder. The hospitality provided me and my colleague that day was awe inspiring. I will never know the full extent of their selfless act. I do know that I felt completely safe and at peace while with them—I knew I was in God's hands.

I realized something further. They had stepped forward to assist us when we were lost, but the cross had made a huge difference. In the presence of the cross, hospitality became a deeper and more profound act and, looking back, the food had been a fundamental part of their hospitality—an expression of their Christian faith. We were, indeed, all part of the larger community of faith, reaching out to each other with the love and generosity that Christ showed us, and feeding each other as God has fed us, to sustain each other body and soul.

My Cuban Grandparents
by Nelida Mora-Morales, Women's Division Director
(2000-2008)
Iglesia Cristiana Juan Wesley, Metodista Unida
Miami, Florida

Allow me to tell you about my own experiences. Going back to my childhood in Cuba, my food and hospitality-related memories began in my maternal grandparents' home. (My paternal grandparents passed away when I was a baby.) I was their first-born granddaughter and at the same time they were my godparents. They lived in the countryside, but they did not own the land. The whole family worked very hard for a landlord. Regardless of the little they had, they offered whatever they did have to any passer-by in need of rest, food, and water.

I lived in the city but I loved to spend my vacation time with my grandparents. The food they served was mostly what they grew. Sometimes for breakfast it was just a roast sweet potato cooked in their primitive, log-burning stove. While waiting for breakfast, I remember going with my *abuelo* (grandfather) to milk the one cow he owned, and what a delicious drink that fresh milk was after it was boiled. We usually had cornmeal for lunch. My *abuela* (grandmother) made it in different combinations with whatever she had available like milk, beans, or lard, and with sugar for dessert. Dinner was a little bit better with rice and beans and sometimes, but not too often, some kind of meat. When any neighbor in the area killed an animal like a pig or cow, they shared with each other because there was no way to preserve the meat for a long time. The best meal was on Sunday because it was chicken prepared in different ways, though not in abundance.

Each person was given a little piece that had to be shared very carefully.

It was really great when we had seasonal fruits! Mangoes and oranges were my favorites. I loved to go under trees and grab the fruit. Those were the best snacks!

Going to the nearby town was not easy. It was a long walk on a dirt road to get to the highway to then wait, sometimes for a long time, for public transportation. So it was not easy to get other things to eat or drink. In spite of the difficulties and the little they had to offer, their hospitality was amazing.

As I mentioned before, like Abraham, my grandparents rushed to serve strangers because their home was a resting place for those passing by. I forgot to mention that they did not have a well, so, in order to have fresh water, it had to be brought from the river that was far away. They had oxen to pull a cart holding a barrel of water. The water was then filtered through pebbles and rocks and deposited in a large, earthen jar.

When the first missionaries traveled to those remote places, they brought spiritual faith food to my relatives. They brought the gospel and my family was fed the Word of God. They accepted Jesus as their Savior. At the same time, those missionaries were nourished by the food and hospitality given to them by my relatives. I remember how they enjoyed the tamales made with corn and other available food.

Somewhere under the cross we changed from strangers to guests—an amazing transformation that can only happen in the presence of the cross. In our Christian faith, guests and strangers are two sides of the same coin, for we all are one in Christ Jesus.

The word hospitality comes from the Greek word, *hospes*, which means a host or a guest. The *Oxford English Dictionary* defines hospitality as "the friendly and generous treatment of guests or strangers."

Most people mean opening their homes when they talk about hospitality. It is about inviting people into the place where we live our lives—our living rooms, dining rooms, and kitchens. We tend to open our homes more easily to family and friends. L. Shannon Jung calls this "everyday" hospitality in his book, *Sharing Food.*

When we seek to open our private spaces to those beyond our closest community, it requires an invitation. This kind of hospitality often takes planning and preparation. Our homes must be presentable for the guests to be received. The preparation for inviting others into your home can be quite a project in the midst of our busy lives. Vacuuming, dusting, mopping—all kinds of cleaning must be done. And then there is also the cooking and arranging of schedules to ensure that the guests are as welcome as possible.

This kind of hospitality is more often called "entertaining" for those of us in the US. It is the opportunity to be the host. We invite business colleagues and other acquaintances to build relationships for the future. These are opportunities to put our best foot forward, for our guests to see us at our best. Our focus is not just our guests but how our guests perceive us. While this kind of hospitality is an important part of our lives, it is not the kind of hospitality that works to build the larger community—the community of Christ.

It is when we move beyond our own barriers that we are open to encounter Christ. Christian hospitality is one of the fullest expressions of our faith because we open ourselves to communion with the entire population of God's family.

Funeral Dinners
by Marilyn Zehring, Women's Division Director

In Matthew 25, Jesus says, "Truly I tell you, just as you did not do it to one of the least of these, you did not do it to me" (Matthew 25:45). One of the ways women of the church answer the call Jesus gives them is by serving funeral dinners to grieving families. During the last few years both our daughter and my mother died unexpectedly. The following days were a time of continual decision making. The funeral dinner was one decision we did not need to make as we knew the women of our church were there for us. At that moment of time we were "one of the least."

Funeral dinners are a time when faith and food come together. Many churches have special funeral casseroles; others have sandwich and salad buffets, and some have dessert and coffee. In my local church of nearly one thousand members each woman is part of a funeral dinner committee with two chairpersons for each committee. Twenty to thirty dinners are served each year. Committee members are asked to provide either a salad or cake. Other members spend around four hours setting up the room, preparing the rest of the food, serving the meal, and finally cleaning up.

A very small United Methodist Church in northeast Nebraska is practicing radical hospitality. Even as the church struggles to remain open, the members have made serving funeral dinners their church's mission. The church becomes a sanctuary for families returning to the community with deceased relatives for burial in the local cemetery. Following the burial the church's fellowship hall becomes a place for the family and friends to gather together in their grief, to remember the deceased, to begin a time of healing, and to join in fellowship together.

The gratefulness felt by the grieving families makes the preparation and serving of the meal truly a time of living out our faith through the hospitality of food.

I remember the weekly dinners I shared at the Wesley Foundation during my college years. It was exciting to put together a meal to share with my friends. Just the act of preparing the food was a time of community. Today, groups of college students still gather to feast and be in fellowship with one another. At Hendrix College in Conway, Arkansas, students engage in weekly meals. One of the students says, "I have come to realize what I like to call the 'uniting power of food,' or the unique moments of sharing that arise out of the offering of hospitality to strangers, and through the simple act of eating together in the same place, at the same moment."[1] Another student shares, "Food is a vital part of offering hospitality to others. . . .We believe that sharing food invites Christ to be among us."[2]

Hospitality is not just being kind to our family and friends; we are to serve our neighbors—wherever and whoever they may be. For when hospitality is shared from the center of our Christian faith there is a "critical shift from *serving* Christ in our neighbor to *meeting* Christ in our neighbor."[3] We met Christ in our neighbors the day my husband and I moved into our new home. Our next-door neighbor brought us a hot, home-cooked meal accompanied with disposable plates and utensils. The eggplant parmigiana, made from ingredients fresh from their garden, spoke volumes. It said, "Welcome to the neighborhood! We know you are exhausted and can't find a thing, so we wanted to help start off your life here in a good way." Their hospitality helped us to feel more at home in our own house. It was a gift of friendship and welcome that meant more to us than words could say. It was a glimpse of Christ.

We are keenly aware of the need for Christ's presence in times of extreme joy or crisis. In many churches, there are a groups of women whose special ministry is hospitality in such times. They provide food to families who have had a death or birth in the family. With this service they bring God's loving presence into homes. When my mother died suddenly, the church community surrounded us with love and comfort. While I don't remember all the people who reached out during that time, I did get glimpses of Christ. I remember the food that came every day to sustain my family during our time of grief. I thank God for the comfort and presence those gifts of food represented.

The comfort that hospitality provides at these times is palpable. Recently a friend wrote to tell me about the results of a family surgery. "Now that we are back home, there are lots of neighbors and church folk who will be visiting, bringing food here, going shopping for us, or providing transportation, that sort of thing—good support." This kind of good support not only helped my friend and her family, it gave me great comfort to know that, although I could not be there for her, she was receiving the support I knew she needed. The body of Christ was providing for her needs.

There is virtually no known culture that does not place great significance on hospitality—the generous and cordial reception of guests, strangers, and acquaintances alike. Food plays a key role in the expression of hospitality. Hospitality is so important that it is an act of righteousness for the people of the Old Testament.[4] Visitors—whether they be friend or foe—were welcomed, fed, lodged, and their animals cared for.

The ancient hospitality of the Israelites and other Middle Eastern nomads was in many ways a survival technique. There were no stores or inns to provide shelter, water, or food as people moved from place to place. Providing hospitality to others meant that when *you* were traveling, equal hospitality would be provided in turn. It was a basic concept on which the ancient world was built. Strict codes of conduct were understood and kept. The alternative was hardship, dishonor, and even death.

The message that Jesus brought to the world refined and clarified the understanding of hospitality. The expression of hospitality becomes more than a method of survival; it becomes an expression of God's love—an expression that need not ever be repaid.

The New Testament is full of stories of the hospitality that Jesus enjoyed as part of his ministry. Particularly in the Gospel of Luke, Jesus is regularly found at table as guest or host. As he traveled with his disciples, people opened their homes to provide shelter, food, and fellowship. Christ transformed hospitality by opening his table to everyone. "Surely his practice of eating with every kind of person—his closest friends, the disciples, Samaritan women, tax collectors, and the disreputable—stands as a witness to the centrality of hospitality to the gospel."[5]

In the early church, each meal was an act of communion with God and with each other. Any act of breaking bread carried with it the remembrance of God's grace through Christ. The hospitality of early Christians was well-known and admired by people of other faiths and practices. Christians did not just reach out to members of their own faith. They reached out to all in need. This was particularly apparent during the many plagues that swept the Roman Empire during the first century. While the multitudes fled in the face of disease, many Christians stayed and provided hospitality, tending the ill at great risk to themselves. As Christians, yesterday and today, "we are not permitted to separate our love of God from our love for others."[6] We serve others as we would serve God. Mortimer Arias, professor of mission and evangelism, credits hospitality as one of the key reasons that Christianity spread so widely and quickly in the first century. One Roman emperor was so impressed "that he commanded his provincial governors to begin practicing hospitality like that of the Christians, if they wanted their empire to grow and remain civil."[7]

Elsewhere in the Bible we are further schooled on hospitality. First Peter 4:9 says, "Be hospitable to one another without complaining." Romans 12:13 says, "Contribute to the needs of the saints; extend hospitality to strangers."

Hospitality is a natural expression of our Christian faith. "It mirrors God's own hospitality and makes family out of strangers."[8] Sara Covin Juengst describes hospitality as a "holy duty."[9] This holy duty cannot be avoided or ignored if we are followers of Christ. Actually we are given very clear instructions on hospitality. We are to reach beyond our comfort zone and serve all of God's family a helping of God's love in the form of food and fellowship—hospitality.

Internationally renowned priest and author Henri Nouwen wrote, "if there is any concept worth restoring to its original depth and evocative potential, it is the concept of hospitality. It is one of the richest biblical terms that can deepen and broaden our insight in our relationships to our fellow human beings."[10]

In order to broaden our insight into our holy duty, we must comprehend the intent and breadth of God's hospitality. It is a vision larger than we can understand for God's vision and its plan takes in more than our family and friends or our church. It is the vision of the banquet where everyone is fed.

> When you give a luncheon or a dinner, do not invite your friends or your brothers or your relatives or rich neighbors, in case they may invite you in return, and you would be repaid. But when you give a banquet, invite the poor, the crippled, the lame, and the blind. And you will be blessed, because they cannot repay you, for you will be repaid at the resurrection of the righteous (Luke 14:12a-13).

God's hospitality is "a matter of justice as well as of love."[11] It is not enough to feed the people who we regularly invite to our table. True hospitality is when all people are fed. God has given us bounty beyond compare; it is our responsibility to enable this bounty to be effectively distributed to all of God's family. This is the point at which humanity has failed humanity and God.

An African Hausa proverb says, "God gives blessings to all people. If people were to distribute them, many would go without."[12] People are not as generous with blessings as God is—and as a result, many go without. How do we extend our hospitality beyond our own experience? When does our relationship with God as reflected in our relationship with food move from the personal and communal into social justice?

Jesus would say that there is no difference between our relationship with God and our relationship with all God's family when in Matthew 25, he praises us when we tend to the sick, hungry, imprisoned—"the least of these." Jesus also rebukes us when we do not reach out beyond our intimate communities. "Lord, when was it that we saw you hungry or thirsty or a stranger or naked or sick or in prison, and did not take care of you?" (Matthew 25:45). Perhaps another way to say this is, "Lord, if I had known it was you, I would have reached out. If I had known it was you and not the homeless person that always sleeps in the doorway, I would have given you whatever your need." Jesus responds, "That was my brother/sister. If you had reached out, you would have glimpsed my face."

The Wodaabe tribe in Niger has a proverb that says, "Your guest is your God."[13] The Wodaabe tradition of hospitality welcomes visitors into their camp. "You take a mat for him to the west of your camp. You take him water to drink. You light a fire for him even if it is not cold. You take him food. Even if you yourself do not like your guest, when his foot comes to your camp, you go to welcome him as if he were your God."[14]

I think the Wodaabe have it right. Jesus treated everyone as he would treat himself. When Jesus looked at another person the first thing he saw was not gender or ethnicity or religion. He saw the God that was in everyone. Hospitality is not limited to our circle of comfort.

God demands radical hospitality[15]—sometimes known as social justice—as the expression of our deep need for God's love in our lives.

Following Christ is a journey full of struggle and reward. John Wesley modeled this journey with his tireless efforts to stand with and for the poor. By reaching out to the poor and giving them a sense of value and worth and reminding them that they too were children of God, Wesley finally began to experience the sense of salvation and forgiveness and peace that he had been seeking so desperately.[16] We, too, can experience that same deep communion with God when we reach out to others. Whether we are next door or around the world, each of us has an opportunity to offer radical hospitality and make a difference in the lives of others.

Mohandas Gandhi framed this notion very succinctly. "To a man with an empty stomach food is God."[17] When we extend our hospitality to the poor and hungry, we offer them God. We offer them love and self-esteem. We offer them physical and spiritual nourishment and our own spirits are fed as well. "Hospitality is finally a life-giving practice"[18] for both the host and the guest.

The church has long been in the forefront of efforts developed to address the needs of the poor and hungry. The United Methodist Church, with its grounding in social justice, has kept the needs of the poor at the center of its mission. The United Methodist connection facilitates the ability of people in the local congregation to work locally, regionally, and globally. As United Methodists, we are uniquely able to reach beyond our own homes and lives and be the hands of Christ to comfort the poor and vulnerable.

Bishop Robert T. Hoshibata (Oregon-Idaho Conference) launched a conference-wide campaign to end hunger in early 2006. Besides feeding the hungry, local churches were called upon to pray, study, dialogue, educate, and advocate. Trinity United Methodist Church in southeast Portland was already deeply engaged in hunger ministry. Each month, a group of women prepares meals for homeless youth. Members work with the Oregon Food Bank and donate food to a local emergency food service provider. Members were asked to bring a pound of food for each day of Lent. On Easter Sunday, they consecrated more than 1,235 pounds of food. Many congregations are joining in to eliminate hunger in their conferences with food pantries, weekly meals, community gardens, summer lunch programs, and more. A special offering at the 2006 annual conference collected well over $21,000 for the Idaho Food Bank. United Methodists are contacting their legislators to change state laws and policies and the enthusiasm grows.

Groups across the US participate in Souper Bowl Sunday by gathering food items and monetary gifts on the day of the Super Bowl. Groups are also encouraged to do a hands-on mission project the previous day. One youth director from Michigan says, "Since we started doing Souper Bowl five years ago, the group has actually wanted to do more throughout the year, other projects and mission work. It's really nurtured them as Christians."[19]

The actions of the Oregon-Idaho Conference and the youth groups in Michigan illustrate a variety of ways in which we can extend hospitality "to the least of these." Opportunities to engage in radical hospitality are readily available when we respond to the physical and spiritual satisfaction God provides us. When we open ourselves to God's hospitality, we become more hospitable to others. Nourished body and soul, we are able to build and strengthen our immediate community and reach out into the larger community. Like the early Christians, others will notice and seek to experience the love we have to share.

If we are to reach out to others in radical hospitality, we need to be able to receive that same hospitality in turn. Reciprocity is an essential part of Christian hospitality. It is a part of hospitality that is often overlooked.

We have been taught from childhood that "it is better to give than to receive." And that is indeed true. Giving to others freely and with a joyful heart is a hard lesson to learn. As we grow in maturity and in faith, we understand that giving is a good and noble thing. We take pride in giving out of our many blessings. We have learned lessons of generosity and hospitality.

Giving to those less fortunate is our charge. We are the hosts for we have been richly blessed. We have grown comfortable with our role as host. Being a host is a position of power; one we want for ourselves. We like being powerful. We enjoy having what others need and then graciously bestowing our bounty on others.

Perhaps we have grown too comfortable with the role of host. We are too comfortable when we can no longer receive. How would you be able to judge your level of comfort? One way to tell would be to take a plate after you have completed your urgent duties at a soup kitchen and go sit and eat with the people you have just served. Take a meal to a shut-in and let them serve you coffee or tea. Hospitality is an act of righteousness that honors our mutual dependency. As we honor each other we honor God.

When asked, "How should our mission and service organizations begin to share the gospel with other indigenous people?" Salustiano Lopez, a Toba Indian and church leader from the Argentine Chaco area, paused for a moment and replied, "I would go and eat their food."[20] If we want to offer Christ, we need to be able to receive Christ. "Eating the food a host offers communicates trust and acknowledges the value of what others have to give."[21] To be a guest is to acknowledge that the host has something to offer. By eating others' food, we show respect and acceptance. It is the same respect and acceptance that God gives each of us—the gift of grace. If we cannot truly offer this to each other, then we cannot truly create the community of faith that reflects our relationship with God.

In our culture, though, it is not always easy to accept hospitality when it is offered. We do not want to seem needy or use the host's minimal resources or even be required to return the favor. Accepting hospitality in the US is difficult and often done reluctantly. This reluctance can be viewed as disrespectful of the host.

I know a man who is a great giver! He will give you a ride home on a rainy day even if it is out of his way. He won't just bring your dinner, he will bring you enough dinner for the entire week. He is also the worst receiver. I can hear him now. "Oh, you didn't have to do that. That's a lot of trouble. No, give that to someone else, I am fine." His resistance to receiving is maddening because people want to thank him. They want to respond not because they need to but because they want him to know they appreciate his selfless, ready generosity. I think he loses an important part of hospitality by not being able to receive. He misses Christ reaching out to him.

To accept bounty from another is a humbling experience. A humble heart is able to acknowledge its vulnerabilities and freely offer up the power that comes with bounty from another. It is what Jesus meant when he washed the feet of the disciples. There is no difference between the rich and the poor, bounty and scarcity, the powerful and the weak. God loves each of us with our individual gifts and failings. When we reach out in love to others, it is that same love that we offer and receive.

Humility is not always a comfortable emotion. Being uncomfortable is something that those of us in North America actively avoid. Therefore, opportunities to receive from others are not sought after. I have found those moments when I must accept hospitality from another in humility to be a deeply rewarding spiritual experience. Many have had similar experiences.

To avoid the necessity of receiving hospitality from a much poorer family in Lesotho, Tina Bohn went late one afternoon to visit a school teacher friend. "Another guest also dropped in and the three of us visited around the kitchen table. Then my friend excused herself and began preparing food. I assumed she was preparing supper for her two young sons who were playing in the yard and thought I should leave so they could eat. But before I could stand up, she brought two plates of food and set them before us. Each plate was filled with *papa* (the thick corn porridge that is a daily staple), pumpkin, a slice of tomato, and a nice piece of chicken. My friend probably had only enough meat for her family, and now she had given two-thirds of it to her unexpected guests. 'I've been wanting to do this for a long time,' she said to me."[22] The pleasure of offering hospitality and food to others is not dampened because of scarcity. The gift of food is made more meaningful by scarcity and must be received humbly by body and spirit.

Whether host or hosted, participating in hospitality is an essential part of our faith. Sharing the food that nourishes our bodies, also shares the source of all good things. It shares God and God's love for each of us.

God's hospitality is available to all. There are no limits on the welcome and nourishment. The table is open. Each of us has supped at God's table and has been sustained in body and spirit.

Myrtis Parker serves as UMW conference president and chief cookie wrangler.

"This has been a great opportunity for our conference to join together for a common cause."

Myrtis Parker, United Methodist Women's president of the Central Texas Annual (regional) Conference and a member of St. Andrew's United Methodist Church, Fort Worth, Texas, says the work and mission of UMW "can't be beat."

The true purpose of United Methodist Women is caring for women and children. "Many people don't realize that that's the major purpose of United Methodist Women, working to make the lives of women and children better," she says.

"I've been in the Methodist Church since birth, even before it was United Methodist," she says. "My mom was in the Methodist Women's organization and she carried me around with her everywhere she went."

The organization has also provided Parker with an opportunity to "get to know like-minded women and establish relationships with them."

"It's provided spiritual development for me, leadership training for me, more of an education on missions and what women's needs are around the world."

Parker will end her four-year term as president just as her home conference hosts the biggest event of the denomination—General Conference. More than one thousand delegates from around the world will gather at the Ft. Worth Convention Center, just eight miles from her home, and make major decisions in the life of The United Methodist Church. Myrtis will be there, too, for ten days of deliberation and celebration.

"Oh yes, I'm a delegate. I was an alternate delegate last time, and I went to Pittsburgh for a little while and I saw the cookies. And I mean, if you were late you didn't get a cookie."

A cookie?

Traditionally, it has fallen to the United Methodist Women's groups of the host conference to supply the denomination's largest legislative body with cookie fuel.

Cookies are baked and brought to the conference center for the 1,000 delegates and hundreds of other visitors to munch on during breaks in debates and discussion on church policy.

Laughing, Parker says, "You know this is Texas so we're called cookie wranglers down here."

The Texas Cookie Wranglers are busy rounding up 1,200 dozen cookies in time for the April 23 opening of the conference.

Even though cookie baking isn't on the official list of chores for United Methodist Women, Parker says when you need something done it is natural "to take it to an organized group of women."

"We just have faith that these great ladies in Texas will get this done. You know, this is the biggest and the best. So we have to do it. It's just a challenge. And I just know we can meet the challenge."

"One can view cookies as healthy depending on the ingredients, and that provides an opportunity for communion in that we join each other in breaking bread and drinking beverages as a community of God's people. And we can all agree on it. We have the opportunity for fellowship, and I think this is good for the soul."

For Myrtis Parker, and United Methodist Women in churches all across the Central Texas Conference, the ingredients they mix and put into their ovens will become more than a treat; they will become food for the soul, a sweet grace for those who deliberate, and celebrate, and contemplate the church of the future.

United Methodist News Service, April 14, 2008. Used by permission.

Our challenge is to show the same gracious hospitality to others. God calls us to reach beyond ourselves and share the bounty we have received with friends, family, and our everyday community. We are glad to do this even in our busy lives.

Still Christ calls us to move beyond our comfort, and find Christ in "the least of these." And when we find Christ in our neighbors near and far, we are to take a moment and truly receive: "For it is in giving that we receive."[23]

It is this mystery of God's love that offers us surprises of love and insight. For it is always possible that by providing succor to a stranger, one may attend an angel unaware. We may find ourselves like the disciples in Luke who "recognized [Jesus] in the breaking of the bread" (Luke 24:35, American Standard Version).

Faith and Food
by Sandra Ruby, former staff of Women's Division

As a small child, the best of both faith and food came together for me in one place—a small clapboard, country church in central Indiana. My fondest childhood memories are of carry-in dinners in church basements, laughing women, and the fragrance permeating the room as the table was loaded with the most delectable cuisine. After the pastor blessed the food (with a prayer that was always too long) folks formed a line, piled plates high with food, and sat down together for a family meal.

The carry-in meals and church suppers we had were reminiscent of the meals Jesus shared with his friends and followers. He relied on the generous hospitality of others, always inviting everyone to feast and fellowship together. My Dad loved these dinners. He would not have used the word "hospitality," but he understood that these meals with sisters and brothers of the faith were related to his idea of the "kin-dom" of God. These were kin folk and we were related as the family of God.

The 1940s were my early childhood years. These years came on the heels of the Great Depression. Every family in our farming community was struggling to make ends meet. We made do with what we had, worked hard each day to make a living, and were thankful for the blessings we were given.

During this time, many young, jobless men walked or hitched a ride across the country searching to find work. These men, sometimes referred to as "hobos," often knocked on our door. My resourceful mother invited them in and then would put together a hearty, hot meal for each one. In addition, she packed a bag or box with sandwiches, fruit, and a slice of pie to sustain the man on his journey. No one was turned away. Sometimes mother's generosity made a difference in what we had for our meals. The menu changed or we received smaller portions.

In my community no one went hungry. In our small community, there were few secrets. The neighborhood woman knew as much about our family as she did her own. The advantage of this was that if you knew, you shared. Vegetables from gardens in summer would be given to neighbors. A sack of tomatoes, onions, or potatoes would be placed on the front step. Apples, pears, cherries, or other fruit of the season would be delivered without fanfare. As each one shared from her/his abundance, all were able to have plenty.

When illness or trouble hit a family, the gift would be a casserole, a pot of soup, or a berry cobbler, usually arriving about mealtime. As a child growing up, I knew that it was a part of our family life to share. It might be a matter of taking some of the beans and corn bread to the old couple up the road, or macaroni and cheese and a loaf of freshly baked bread shared with the family across the way who had six children. The widow next door, who popped in regularly and usually around mealtime, was always invited to sit at our table.

Holidays were an additional opportunity to share, and I remember one cold and snowy Christmas morning my mother announced that my brother and I were to deliver "goodies." We objected. It was Christmas and we wanted to play. Mother made us understand that Christmas was a celebration of the great gift of the Christ Child from God. It was important that we share with those who had less; then we could have our Christmas.

My family home was next to the church, so it was assumed that we were connected with the church. We were. My father was the Class Leader in our United Brethren tradition, which meant that he carried the responsibility for much of the work of our church in the absence of the pastor who served three other small churches. The foundation of my faith is based on what I watched my mother and father live each day.

The church in this Midwestern farming community was the center for all of the passages of life: weddings, baby showers, anniversaries, Christmas parties, bazaars, graduations, Thanksgiving feasts, and funerals. All of these gatherings required food.

Church suppers served many purposes. One was for fund-raising. These funds were for missions, church repairs, or to assist a family in need. My favorite was the chicken and noodle dinner. Everyone had a specialty. My mother and grandmother were the super noodle makers. Other women in the church specialized in green beans, mashed potatoes, pies, cakes, or biscuits.

Two days before the big event, grandma came to our house early in the morning. Dozens of eggs, sacks of flour, big bowls, rolling pins, and waxed paper were used. As the noodles were made and rolled to form thin platters of dough, they were laid out on flat surfaces to dry. Every flat surface in our house, including the beds covered with bleached sheets, had drying noodle dough. Kids were banned from the house. We picnicked on peanut butter and jelly sandwiches and Kool-Aid sitting on the front porch.

On the big day, all of the women were in the church basement early to set up. On the surface, it seemed to be folks cooking a meal. It was far more than this. These folks, mostly women, were sharing the best they had to offer: food from their own pantries, skills in food preparation, support for one another, and satisfying work for the greater good of the community. With hands in dishwater, they bragged about their children, announced with joy the expected arrival of grandchild, shared their daily struggle, and adjustment with the recent death of a spouse. Good humor and gentle teasing were a part of the conversation. It was an interchange of faith journeys.

Hospitality, at its best, provides for the well-being of each person without demands or restrictions: giving while receiving. Over the steaming stove, friendships were made which lasted a lifetime. There in the church basement, while preparing food for others, women were nourished spiritually. It was the compassionate therapy needed to strengthen these women to survive the rigors of their days.

Funeral dinners were the most awesome of the dinners for me as a child. The celebration of life mixed with grief permeated the preparation of this family meal. When a person of the community died, a feast would be provided for the family and friends in the church basement after the service in the sanctuary. The menu included all of the comfort foods. Calorie counting and caution about cholesterol were not a consideration.

This was the time to surround the family with our compassion. It was an attempt to follow the example of Jesus and to share what we had to offer for healing and giving hope. The meal was served to everyone in the community. This was one way to tell the bereaved family about God. God is love. God is generous. God is always with us. God offers us nourishment and comfort when we need it most.

Today, I have not moved theologically so far from the place in which I lived as a child. When a new neighbor moves in, a plate of cookies is an introduction and welcome. When a friend is ill, a casserole is my way of saying, "I am praying for you and your family."

Faith and food are closely related—even blended. They are both integral to holy hospitality. Faith and food both offer sustenance and provide strength for the journey. True hospitality is the sharing of the good news and our love of Jesus the Christ. It is offering ourselves along with a pie, salad, or casserole, saying, "I care enough to give you the very best I have."

Food in the African-American Tradition
by Faye Wilson

I grew up on a small, 20-acre farm in the southeastern most part of Maryland—a rural region called Delmarva, a peninsula which consisted of tracts of land that were part of the states of Delaware, Maryland, and Virginia. Seemingly everyone had a small farm or worked on someone else's larger farm.

I grew up in a large family, one of 12 children. As you can imagine, a lot of our attention was focused on some aspect of food. One thing I learned right away was that food was to be blessed. Our father, as head of the household, most often said the grace that included a plea for the "nourishment and strength of our bodies." Whether we ate at school or consumed sandwiches and Kool-Aid from the back of our station wagon, we were to say "thanks" over our food.

I think we invented the concept of tailgate parties. We grew up in church. We were the largest family in St. John's Holiness Church where our mom was the assistant pastor and eventually became the pastor. We fellowshipped regularly with other small Pentecostal churches like our own. Church anniversaries were a special event in the life of each church, and they were usually observed with afternoon and evening services—with a meal served in the church dining hall in between. For a long time we Wilson children were not allowed to eat in the dining room as my mom thought there were too many of us, and we packed our lunch and ate out of the back of our station wagon.

Eventually, one mother convinced my mom that there was enough to feed the Wilson brood and we partook of the heavily laden tables of fried chicken, chicken and dumplings, turnip greens, green beans, and desserts. The preparation of church suppers was a ritual and my first experience with potluck suppers. Each family brought a dish, and there always seemed to be more than enough. As I grew up, I worked in the kitchen or the dining hall—serving food, clearing tables, washing dishes. I learned that every feast called for a lot of hard work—and great fellowship.

Like every meal in my life, these church fellowship dinners required grace: a sung grace. Once all the food was ready, someone would strike up the song: "Come and dine, the Master's calling, come and dine; you may feast at Jesus' table all the time; he who fed the multitude, turned the water into wine, to the hungry calling now—come and dine." (I later learned that it was a hymn in the songbook *Gospel Pearls*.) I remember the words and tune to this day. My first songwriting venture was to create a gospel arrangement of that song for our youth choir.

Food was sacred. While abundant (at least to me, since we grew and preserved a lot of our food [including killing a hog every January and shooting a deer on occasion]), it was never to be wasted. I was an early member of the "clean plate club." At our church suppers we would hear: "take all you want, but eat all you take."

The absence of food was sacred too. In my church tradition, fasting was taught and practiced as a spiritual discipline. We had not one but two fast days each week: Tuesdays and Fridays. Fasting began with your last meal the night before and continued until at least 3:00 p.m. the following day. Fasting was to be done whether you went to school or went to work in the fields. Our church practiced a "no food or drink" (not even water) type of fasting. I remember someone having an occasional headache but I don't recall anyone becoming ill. It was just what we did as a way of expressing our devotion to the Lord.

At least once a year, usually at its beginning, we had "shut-in" or "tarry" services, when the faithful would go to the church to participate in an extended fast (usually five to seven days). Participating meant sleeping at the church (with prayer every three hours—even during the night) and going without food and water. If a person began to feel weak, she or he could suck on ice chips. Again, this denying oneself food—or turning your plate down—was a spiritual practice of seeking direction from God for one's life.

Communion was also a spiritual discipline of my growing-up years. I can remember my mom making unleavened bread and also washing and ironing those white, white Communion table cloths. A long table was set up in the front of the church and chairs were put around it. Only those who professed salvation were asked to sit around the table. I can still remember the excitement and awe I felt when at last I could come to the table and eat the hard, crumbly bread and drink grape juice out of little glass cups.

My great food experiences were not limited to church. We also had great family gatherings. In my household, birthdays might pass by without a cake and candles, but holidays were to be observed. Christmas, Fourth of July, and Labor Day were always observed with food. Thanksgiving was special indeed. Even now I marvel that so many of us fit in our childhood home—especially as my siblings married and had families. My favorite was my mother's oyster fritters. As some left the table, another group sat down, and we washed and dried plates, flatware, and glasses in the kitchen in between servings.

My personal stories are a small glimpse of the role of food in an African-American family. One story involved sharing our table with the traveling preacher man. My grandmother Clara Wilson, the keeper of memories in our families, talked about how the preacher came to dinner on Sunday, the only day of the week they would have fried chicken. Naturally, the children had to wait until the grown-ups had finished before they could eat. She sat on the stairs, watching the good Reverend talk and eat and eat and talk. Dismay descended upon her as she saw the platter of fried chicken dwindle. As she saw the preacher go back one more time, her frustration broke forth and she cried out, "Not the last piece of fried chicken!" Needless to say, she went to bed without any supper that night!

In the African-American tradition, we are known for our

soul food: chitlings, macaroni and cheese, fried chicken, collard greens, corn bread, hopping john (rice and beans), smothered pork chops, to name a few items. Eating a soul food dinner is extremely important at New Year's. Many African-American families leave Watch Night Service (on December 31st) to go to a feast that must include collard greens (eaten for financial success in the new year), chitlings, black-eyed peas, and pig feet.

The sharing and consumption of food in the African-American tradition is not without tension. For a significant part of our history we were denied food in public spaces. Those of my parents' generation knew what it was like to travel by public transportation (buses and trains) or ride in private cars with lunch packed carefully in shoeboxes lined with waxed paper or carried in paper sacks. It was not just about saving money; in certain areas of our country, there was simply no place where an African American could stop to purchase a meal.

This lack of public access to food as well as the practice of demanding that African Americans not share a table in public with white Americans, paved the way for the lunch counter sit-ins which were part of the civil rights protests in the early 1960s. What a powerful link between food and faith: believing that all people are created equal, and that God does not desire people to be separated based on the color of their skin.

Food continues to be part of the political- and community-building process. In the early 1960s, Dr. Maulena Karenga founded the practice of Kwanzaa. I began observing Kwanzaa in the late 1970s while a student at Drew Theological School and have observed this tradition ever since, holding many celebrations. The karamu (or feast) is generally held on the sixth day of Kwanzaa. It is an opportunity for people to prepare foods (store-bought items are not recommended) which are shared around a common table.

In a tradition that African Americans share with many other cultures and nationalities, food connects us and comforts us in the passing of loved ones. When my brother Charles died in January 2007, friends and loved ones of my sister Rosie and mine (we had been his caretakers) brought food day after day. Some prepared an entire meal and came to share it with us. Even when grief and shock took our appetites, the gathering around our table, sharing food so lovingly and prayerfully prepared, brought forth healing in our souls.

Ultimately, that is the purpose of breaking bread together—whether in the Communion ritual or in our homes—to nourish our physical bodies and to sustain our souls. It is the creation and sharing of memories that enrich our lives.

*Faye Wilson, Ed.D. is a member of Mt. Zion United Methodist Church, Quantico, Maryland, where she is vice-president of her UMW unit, coordinates a praise dancers group, and works in the music ministry. She worked as a mission educator for 21 years for the General Board of Global Ministries. In addition to writing mission study material, she writes for **Response** magazine.*

CHAPTER 4

Feasting and Fasting

"Quickly, bring out a robe—the best one—and put it on him; put a ring on his finger and sandals on his feet. And get the fatted calf and kill it, and let us eat and celebrate; for this son of mine was dead and is alive again; he was lost and is found!" And they began to celebrate (Luke 15:22-24).

T he father in this passage from Luke's Gospel is not just throwing a feast because his son has come home. He throws the feast because the son who had broken his heart, who he thought he would never see again, the son he thought was dead, had come home. The fatted calf was not just killed to serve at the feast. The calf was a sacrifice to God to express earnest and sincere thanks.[1] Thanking God was the father's first thought after welcoming his son home.

These moments of pure, profound joy are few and far between in our lives. These moments are meant to be shared. A Swedish proverb captures this emotion: "Shared joy is a double joy; shared sorrow is half a sorrow." And who wouldn't want to double their joy? The joy shared fills our hearts with happiness, our souls with satisfaction, and the memories created are carefully kept.

You cannot have a festival, a feast, with only one person. A feast requires a family, a group, a community, and a gathering to share the blessings widely, to expand our joy. Just as the father of the prodigal son gathered everyone nearby, we gather to celebrate. We gather to celebrate in the presence of God.

What do we celebrate in our lives? We celebrate the things that are most important to us—birthdays, weddings, graduations, anniversaries, reunions, homecomings. At these times, we want to thank God and acknowledge that this event is worth remembering.

We celebrate the joy that is in our hearts when special events such as these happen. An announcement or commitment is made public. Someone is honored for their skills and abilities, or is welcomed home after an absence. We mark milestones in our lives and the lives of the people we love. We celebrate the people and the relationships that are blessed and recognized at these moments of feast.

Harvest feasts are common in all cultures as we found in chapter one. In ancient times, the harvest was an outpouring of thankfulness that the community will survive another year. The harvest represented the answer to their great need and the bounty that God provides. These acts of thanks and joy were part of religious expression. The harvest festival in the Old Testament, Sukkot—the Festival of Ingathering—was ordained by God to be held in the early fall. People of the Jewish faith still celebrate the harvest festival by building booths open to the sky, often eating and sleeping in them to remind themselves of their connection to the land and to God. The booths are not supposed to be solid or permanent; rather, their fragility echoes the fragility of our lives.

Along with Sukkot, God called for two other feasts of remembrance and thanksgiving (Exodus 23:14-19). Shavu'ot, the Festival of First Fruits, is held in late spring celebrating the harvest of barley.

Both of these festivals have special foods associated with them. These foods are obvious and relate to the corresponding harvest. But the third feast, Passover, has the most special foods of all.

Passover, which remembers the exodus from Egypt, is quite a feast. But it is a feast full of ritual and teaching. Passover requires specific foods with specific meanings which are described during part of the feast. These foods are used to evoke memories—memories of God's steadfast love.

• Drops of wine symbolize the plagues that afflicted Egypt to convince Pharaoh to let the Israelites go. The drops, removed from the drinking cups, reflect the fact that the joy of the Exodus is diminished by the plagues.

• The lamb is a reminder that God passed over the Israelite houses when the tenth plague was visited upon the Egyptians after the Israelites offered the Passover sacrifice.[2]

• Parsley symbolizes both the humble origins of the Jewish people as well as the rebirth of spring, which starts at the time of Passover.[3]

• The salt water symbolizes the tears shed during slavery.[4] The salt water also represents the Red Sea that was miraculously parted for their escape.

• Charoset is a mixture of nuts, fruit, wine, and spices that symbolizes the mortar used by the Jewish people to make bricks while enslaved in Egypt.[5]

• The bitter herbs, maror, are a reminder of the bitter pain and suffering the Israelites went through as slaves to the Egyptians.[6]

• The matzah represents the hurried Exodus from Egypt when the Israelites left so quickly that their dough did not have time to rise.[7]

- The egg is a symbol of mourning, a reminder that the Temple in Jerusalem is no longer standing. And since it has no beginning and no end, the egg is also a symbol of new life and hope.

This feast, rich in remembrance and ritual, was what Jesus was celebrating with his disciples before he was arrested. The memories evoked for Jesus and the disciples as part of this feast strengthened and prepared them for the coming passion. The Passover ritual is eaten in and around the bountiful meal shared with family and loved ones.

Feasts that celebrate life's rhythms and markers are also celebrated with abundant food. As in the Passover meals, we don't serve just any food. We serve favorite foods, special foods, food infused with significance and meaning. Turkey with all the "fixin's" is the menu for Thanksgiving or Christmas. For many Americans, birthdays and weddings boast special cakes or desserts to celebrate the occasion. The feast to welcome home a soldier would include the soldier's favorites and be shared with gusto with all who gather. The food is what makes the event so jubilant. God is the benefactor for every feast.

A Prophetic Voice in Jewish, Multireligious, and American Life
The Song of Songs as a Sacred Recipe –
For Charoset at the Seder Table
by Rabbi Arthur Ocean Waskow

The Passover Seder literally embodies ideas—by turning them into food. Among these foods we eat are bitter herbs for the bitterness of slavery, unleavened matzah-bread for the haste of turning the bread of the poor into the bread of freedom, greens for the sprouting of new life in springtime.

There is also a dish called charoset, and this one is not explained—in fact, it is mentioned only indirectly—in the written Passover Haggadah, or "Telling." Though unmentioned, undescribed, and unexplained, its necessity is passed on by word of mouth, so strongly that it appears in every Seder throughout the Jewish world. Its precise recipe varies from one Jewish culture to another, but the basics are clear: It is a paste made up of chopped fruit, chopped nuts, spices, and wine.

Charoset is mentioned in the Haggadah only by utter indirection. Four Questions, traditionally asked by the youngest person present, help initiate the Telling of the Passover story of the Exodus of ancient Israel from ancient Egypt. After asking, "How is this night different from all other nights?" the Four Questions point out: "On all other nights, we do not 'dip' even once; on this night, twice."

The first of these two "dippings" is dipping green vegetable in salt water. This is heralded in the sacred text by a blessing for the Source of this fruit of the earth. The second dipping is dipping a piece of matzah in charoset. Participants in the Seder know this, but the text ignores it. There is not even a special blessing for the eating of charoset.

So let us ask the unasked question: "Why is there charoset on the Seder plate?" The conventional answer, written in no Haggadah but transmitted by word of mouth, is that the paste of charoset reminds us of the mortar that Israelite slaves were forced to use to hold together the stones and bricks of Pharaoh's storehouses as they slaved to build them.

But charoset is sweet. If it mimics the mortar of slavery, it must also remind us that slavery may taste sweet, and this is itself a deeper kind of slavery.

There is a still deeper truth, transmitted not by word of mouth but taste of mouth, kiss of mouth. Charoset is an embodiment of the sacred text that is perhaps the most "subversive," certainly the most fully embodied, book of the Hebrew Scriptures—the Song of Songs. Charoset is literally a full-bodied taste of the Song. And Jewish tradition calls for the chanting of the Song during Passover.

The text of the Song subtly, almost secretly, bears the recipe for charoset, and we might well see the absence of any specific written explanation of charoset as itself a subtle, secret pointer toward the "other" liberation of Pesach—the erotic loving freedom celebrated in the Song of Songs, which is perhaps why we are taught to chant it during Passover.

The Song of Songs is sacred not only to Jews, but also to Christians and to Muslims, and especially to the mystics in all three traditions. Its earth-and-human-loving erotic energy has swept away poets and rabbis, lovers and priests, dervishes and gardeners.

Yet this sacred power—"Love is strong as death," sings the Song—has frightened many generations into limiting its power. Redefining its flow as a highly structured allegory, or hiding it from the young, or forbidding it from being sung in "ewine-houses"— what today we would call "night clubs."

Why is this time of year set aside for this extraordinary love poem? At one level, because it celebrates the springtime rebirth of life, when the flowers rise up against winter—just as Passover is a celebration of rebirthing freedom, rising up against Pharaoh.

And the parallel goes far deeper. For the Song celebrates a new way of living in the world.

The way of love between the earth and her human earthlings, beyond the future of conflict between them that accompanies the end of Eden.

The way of love between women and men, with women cel-

ebrated as leaders and initiators, beyond the future of subjuga-
tion of women by men that accompanies the end of Eden.

The way of bodies and sexuality celebrated, beyond the
future of shame and guilt that accompanies the end of Eden.

The way of God so fully present in the whole of life that
God needs no specific naming (for in the Song, God's name is
never mentioned).

The way of adulthood, where there is no parent and there
are no children. No one is giving orders, and no one obeys them.
Rather there are grown-ups, lovers—unlike the domination and
submission that accompany the end of Eden. In short, the garden of the Song of Songs is the Garden of Eden for grown-ups.
For a grown-up human race.

In the beginning, Eden was childhood, bliss that was unconscious, unaware. In the Garden, the human race moves into adolescence—rebelling against Authority, finding sexuality embarrassing. Leaving the Garden is entry to the adult drudgery of
hard work and hierarchy—men bossing women. But in the Song,
the human race grows up into another stage: maturity. Death is
known, conflict is recognized (as when the heroine's brothers
beat her up), yet joy and harmony sustain all.

Now what does it mean to say that the Song of Songs is the
recipe for charoset?

Verses from the Song:

> "Feed me with apples and with raisin-cakes;
> "Your kisses are sweeter than wine;
> "The scent of your breath is like apricots;
> "Your cheeks are a bed of spices;
> "The fig tree has ripened;
> "Then I went down to the walnut grove."

So the "recipe" points us toward apples, quinces, raisins,
apricots, figs, nuts, wine. Within the framework of the free

fruitfulness of the earth, the "recipe" is free-form: no measures, no teaspoons, no amounts. Not even a requirement for apples rather than apricots, cinnamon rather than cloves, figs rather than dates. So there is an enormous breadth for the tastes that appeal to Jews from Spain, Poland, Iraq, India, America.

Nevertheless, I will offer a recipe.

Take a pound of raw shelled almonds, two pounds of organic raisins, and a bottle of red wine. On the side have organic apricots, chopped apples, figs, and dates (no pits), and small bottles of powdered cinnamon, nutmeg, and cloves.

Assemble either an electric blender, or your great-grandmom's cast-iron hand-wound gefilte fish chopper brought from the Old Country. If it's the blender, put it on "chop" rather than "paste" frequency.

Start feeding the almonds and raisins into the blender or mixer, in judicious mixture. (How do you know "judicious"? Whatever doesn't get the whole thing stuck so it won't keep grinding.) Whenever you feel like it, pour in some wine to lubricate the action. Stop the action every once in a while to poke around and stir up the ingredients.

Freely choose when to add apricots, apples, figs, and/or dates. Taste every ten minutes or so. If you start feeling giddy, good! That's the wine.

Add the spices. Clove is powerful, sweet, and subtly sharp at the same time; a lot will get you just on the edge of altered consciousness.

Keep stirring, keep chopping, keep dribbling wine—not till the charoset turns to paste but till there are still nubs of nuts, grains of raisin, and suddenly a dollop of apricot spurting on your tongue.

You say this doesn't seem like a recipe, too free? Ahh—as the Song itself says again and again, "Do not stir up love until it pleases. Do not rouse the lovers till they're willing."

Serve at the Pesach Seder, and also in secret on your wedding night. And on every wedding anniversary. And every once in a while, but not too often, on a night when you want to celebrate and embody your love.

Dad's Favorite Cookies
by Harriett J. Olson, Deputy General Secretary,
Women's Division

"What is Charlie's favorite cookie?" my mom remembers asking. "Molasses. But I don't have a recipe—I just make them," was grandma's response. "I'll have to show you."

My mother was visiting dad's family, meeting them after she and my dad became engaged, and was planning to add some recipes for dad's comfort food to her preparations for married life. She told us that she accepted grandma's invitation and spent an afternoon watching her every step as she made a batch of dad's favorite molasses cookies.

This recipe involved sifting and melting and balling the dough and flattening it in a saucer of sugar. The notecard carrying the recipe had a careful ingredient list and description of steps, but it also had small corrections or elaborations inserted as mom remembered what she saw as well as following the instructions.

"Sift spices together with flour."

"Balls of dough about the size of a walnut."

These gave the sense of the experience as well as the science of the thing.

Of course, when we were children, we also learned to make these cookies. We learned by both watching my mother and attending to her notes from watching grandma—a very smart ploy on my mother's part—one of the few recipes for which I still use the sifter! From generation to generation.

The "balling and flattening" process takes some time. It doesn't involve the "don't talk to me—I'm counting" process of measuring ingredients and it continues while the smells of baking and the first trays of warm cookies reward the participants. This is the time to talk about what events should be in the Christmas letter, who we've already heard from and how their families are, and who we hope to hear from still.

The molasses cookies are not the most brightly colored ones on the tray, or the biggest, and they don't have any jam or chocolate to add to their appeal, but they smell like Christmas and home and family.

In the United States, we enjoy feasting so much that we often eat those foods previously reserved for special occasions in our daily lives. "With abundant resources at our disposal, we eat as though each day were a festival, with fresh fruits and vegetables year-round and desserts every day. But our eating lacks the mirth of a long-awaited, well-deserved holiday."[8] Our joy is diluted and the happiness and fond memories that are derived from the special food no longer satisfies our hearts and souls.

Prairie Hospitality
by Kathleen Becker Enzminger, Women's Division Director
(2000-2008)

My father's family homesteaded in Logan County in what was then Dakota Territory and my father grew up on the farm. He used to talk about how much fun Sunday afternoons were.

Right next door to the farm was a small country church and every Sunday began with church attendance. After church my Grandmother Becker would have a big kettle of chicken noodle soup ready to eat and would invite guests. The family loved company and would invite the preacher, friends, and family. Many times 30 or 40 people would be there, counting children.

Sometimes church was in the afternoon. Then they would come to eat before church. Also served were chicken and dumplings and *Blachinda (bla-jenda)* and *Bruschke (burr-aush-ke)*, which are a kind of baked turnover. *Blachinda* is made with sweet-roll dough and a pumpkin filling, and *Bruschke* is made with bread dough and a cooked mixture of hamburger and sauerkraut filling.

These foods are still served when we have Becker family reunions.

When we seek the special and find only the ordinary, we can find ourselves empty. In some ancient stories, the worst curse is the curse that allows you to eat what you want all the time but the food does not satisfy, the flavors have no taste. This emptiness is more than that of hunger to satisfy the stomach. It is emptiness of the soul.

Psalm 63 begins by describing this emptiness.

A Psalm of David, when he was in the Wilderness
of Judah.

[1]O God, you are my God, I seek you,
my soul thirsts for you;
my flesh faints for you,
as in a dry and weary land where there
is no water.
[2]So I have looked upon you in the sanctuary,
beholding your power and glory.
[3]Because your steadfast love is better than life,
my lips will praise you.
[4]So I will bless you as long as I live;
I will lift up my hands and call on your name.

[5]My soul is satisfied as with a rich feast,
and my mouth praises you with joyful lips
[6]when I think of you on my bed,
and meditate on you in the watches of the night;
[7]for you have been my help,
and in the shadow of your wings I sing for joy.
[8]My soul clings to you;
your right hand upholds me.

[9]But those who seek to destroy my life
shall go down into the depths of the earth;
[10]they shall be given over to the power of the
sword, they shall be prey for jackals.
[11]But the king shall rejoice in God;
all who swear by him shall exult,
for the mouths of liars will be stopped.

King David was used to feasting as a part of his everyday life. It is the privilege of a king to have bountiful resources to command. But when David discovered that his son, Absalom, was planning a coup, he fled into the desert and exile. In the desert he found himself without resources. He was a hungry and thirsty fugitive. Although he had almost no food and no water, David found that his greatest hunger and thirst was for God. In this Psalm, David recognizes that his hunger and thirst could only be satisfied by God. So David seeks God. He doesn't just wait for God or expect that God would reach out to him. He knew that any separation he felt from God was of his own making.

David was so intent on renewing his relationship with God that it occupied his thoughts when he was awake and when he was trying to sleep. He reached out for God in desperation and was rewarded with "a rich feast." This feast satisfied his soul. He was so satisfied and in such deep communion with God that he realized that even death would not remove this absolute divine contentment. He was completely assured of God's love and presence.

David shows us that there are times when, to enjoy the feast that God offers, we must fast.

Fasting

http://gbgm-umc.org/umw/wesley/disciple.stm
• John Wesley fasted two days a week: Wednesdays and Fridays
• Later he dropped his fasting to once a week: Friday

Wesley was convinced that fasting, abstaining from food or drink, was a practice firmly grounded in the Bible. People in Old Testament times fasted (Ezra 8:23). So did Jesus and his followers (Matthew 4:2; Acts 13:3), and Wesley saw no reason why modern Christians should not follow the same pattern. His plan of fasting sometimes allowed for limited eating and drinking. He found that fasting advanced holiness.

John Wesley: Holiness of Heart and Life. Copyright © 1996 Charles Yrigoyen Jr., p. 33.

John Wesley, John Emory. The Works of the Reverend John Wesley, A.M.

T. Mason and G. Lane, for the Methodist Episcopal Church. 1840 SERMON XXVII - Upon our Lord's Sermon on the Mount

Moreover, when ye fast, be not as the hypocrites, of a sad countenance; for they disfigure their faces, that they may appear unto men to fast. Verily I say unto you, They have their reward. But thou, when thou fastest, anoint thy head and wash thy face; That thou appear not unto men to fast, but unto thy Father which is in secret; and thy Father, which seeth in secret, shall reward thee openly. (Matt. vi 16:18) (page 592)

1. I shall endeavor to show first, what is the nature of fasting, and what the several sorts and degrees thereof. As to the nature of it all, the inspired writers, both in the Old Testament and the New take the word to "fast" in one single sense, for not to eat, to abstain from food. This is so clear that it would be labour lost to quote the words of David, Nehemiah, Isaiah, and the prophets which followed, or of our Lord and his apostles; all agreeing in this: that to fast is not to eat for a time prescribed.

2. To this other circumstances were usually joined by them of old, which had no necessary connection with it. Such were the neglect of their apparel, the laying aside those ornaments which they were accustomed to wear; the putting on mourning, the strewing ashes upon their head, or wearing sackcloth next their skin. But we find little mention made in the New Testament of any of these indifferent circumstances; nor does it appear that any stress was laid upon them by the Christians of the purer ages, however some penitents might voluntarily use them as outward signs of inward humiliation. Much less did the apostles or the Christians temporary with them beat or tear their own flesh. Such "discipline" as this was not unbecoming the priests or worshippers of Baal. The Gods of the heathens were but devils and it was doubtless acceptable to their devil-god when his priests (1 Kings xviii 28) "cried aloud and cut themselves after their manner, till the blood gushed out upon them...."

3. As to the degrees or measures of fasting, we have instances of some who have fasted several days together. So Moses, Elijah, and our blessed Lord, being endued with supernatural strength for that purpose are recorded to have fasted without intermission "forty days and forty nights." But the time of fasting more frequently mentioned in Scripture is one day, from morning till evening. And this was the fast commonly observed among the ancient Christians. But beside these they had also their half-fasts (semi-jejunia as Tertullian styles them) on the fourth and sixth days of the week (Wednesday and Friday) throughout the year; on which they took no sustenance till three in the afternoon, the time when they returned from the public service.

4. Nearly related to this is what our Church seems peculiarly to mean by the term "abstinence"; which may be used when we can-

not fast entirely, by reason of sickness or bodily weakness. This is the eating little; the abstaining in part; the taking of a smaller quantity of food than usual. I do not remember any scriptural instance of this. But neither can I condemn it; for the Scripture does not. It may have its use and receive a blessing from God.

5. The lowest kind of fasting, if it can be called by that name, is the abstaining from pleasant food. Of this we have several instances in Scripture, besides that of Daniel and his brethren: who from a peculiar consideration, namely, that they might "not defile themselves with the portion of the king's meat, nor with the wine which he drank" (a "daily provision" of which "the king had appointed for them") "requested" and obtained of "the prince of the eunuchs," pulse to eat, and water to drink. Perhaps from a mistaken imitation of this might spring the very ancient custom of abstaining from flesh and wine during such times as were set apart for fasting and abstinence; if it did not rather arise from a supposition that these were the most pleasant food, and a belief that it was proper to use what was least pleasing at those times of solemn approach to God.

6. In the Jewish church, there were some stated fasts. Such was the fast of the seventh month, appointed by God himself to be observed by all Israel, under the severest penalty. "The Lord spake unto Moses, saying, ...on the tenth day of the seventh month there shall be a day of atonement; ...and ye shall afflict your souls...to make an atonement for you before the Lord your God. For whatsoever soul it be that shall not be afflicted in that same day, he shall be cut off from among his people." (Leviticus 23:26) (pages 594-596)

What are the grounds, the reasons, and ends of fasting?

Those whose souls and minds are deeply engaged, occupied, impatient, depressed.

BIBLICAL EXAMPLES

- Saul distressed with the Philistines who were at war with him and felt God had abandoned him. (1 Samuel 28:15-20)
- Those in the ship with St. Paul continued fasting for fourteen days. (Acts 27:33)
- David fasted in mourning for Saul and his son Jonathan after their deaths in battle. (2 Samuel 1:12)
- St. Paul after he was led into Damascus was three days without sight and did not eat nor drink. (Acts 9:9)
- Asking for redemption for past transgressions.
- To punish themselves for their sins; ex: David wept and chastised his soul with fasting.
- An aid in prayer.
- It is for the ends of averting the wrath of God and obtaining what blessings we need that God appointed fasting. (Jonah 3:4)
- Fasting is a sign of showing humility to God. (p. 601)
- Fasting is used to obtaining blessings. The Israelites fasted from day until evening in order for the Lord to deliver them from the Benjaminites. (Judges 20:26)
- Apostles fasted with Prayer when they desired a blessing on an important undertaking. (Acts 13:1-3, 23) (page 606)

Rev. Wesley, John A.M. Sermons on Several Occasions. *The Works of John Wesley*, Vol. 4, Sermons IV 115-151, edited by Albert C. Outler (Abingdon Press, Nashville, TN: 1987), 94.

It would be easy to show in how many respects the Methodists in general are deplorably wanting in the practice of Christian self denial; from which indeed they have been continually frightened by the silly outcries of the antinomians. To instance only in one. While we were at Oxford the rule of every Methodist was (unless in case of sickness,) to <u>fast</u> every Wednesday and Friday in the year, in imitation of the primitive church, for which they had the highest reverence. Now this practice of the primitive church is universally allowed. "Who does not know," says Epiphanius, an ancient writer, "that the fasts of the fourth and sixth days of the week (Wednesday and Friday) are observed by the Christians throughout the whole world?" So they were by the Methodists for several years; by them all, without any exception. But afterwards some in London carried this to excess, and fasted so as to impair their health. It was not long before others made this a pretence for not fasting at all. And I fear there are now thousands of Methodists, so called, both in England and Ireland, who, following the same bad example, have entirely left off fasting; who are so far from fasting twice in the week (as all the stricter Pharisees did) that they do not fast twice in the month. Yea, are there not some of you who do not fast one day, from the beginning of the year to the end? But what excuse can there be for this? I do not say for those that call themselves members of the Church of England; but for any who profess to believe the Scripture to be THE word of God? Since, according to this, the man that never fasts is no more in the way to heaven than the man that never prays.

David's lifestyle was stripped away. His access to physical pleasure and nourishment abruptly ceased. When everything was gone, his only solace and sustenance was God. And the nourishment that God offered was a feast. "Feasting on God is encountering God in a way that abundantly satisfies our needs.

And the reason David finds satisfaction is because he has moved beneath the surface, past his physical and political needs to the deepest need in all of us: the need for God. At the end of the psalm he's still talking about those who seek to destroy his life; the political and physical problems are still there. But he has connected with his deepest need for God and has beheld God and is satisfied."[9]

While David had this experience thrust upon him, it produced much the same result that many faithful find in fasting. Fasting is a practice that holds great opportunity for refocusing our relationship with God. Fasting is a practice shared by all religions and faith expressions to one degree or another. It was a regular practice for observant Jews in Jesus' time. We find Jesus fasting and praying frequently throughout the Gospels.

Jesus fasted in preparation for his ministry. After Jesus was baptized by John, three of the Gospels report, "He fasted for forty days and forty nights, and afterwards he was famished" (Matthew 4:2, Luke 4:1-2, Mark 1:12). Although Jesus was famished for food at the end of his fast, he was prepared for his ministry. He had communed with God and gained clarity about his ministry. That clarity was gained as much by what he was denied as by what he received. He would not bend to his physical hunger (turning stones into bread). He would not test God; rather, he would be obedient to God's will. For Jesus, obedience to God's will was sustenance.

By Jesus' time, fasting had become commonplace as an act of piety and devotion. On the second and fifth days of the week when the Torah was read, the faithful fasted, because on those days the word of the Lord was their food. Unfortunately, many practitioners became prideful of their careful observation and would indicate their private act to those around them. The purpose of their fasting had moved from spiritual sustenance and had become an ostentatious act of pride in their observance.

When Jesus' disciples asked him to give them instructions on fasting, he responded thus, "And whenever you fast, do not look dismal, like the hypocrites, for they disfigure their faces so as to show others that they are fasting. Truly I tell you, they have received their reward. But when you fast, put oil on your head and wash your face, so that your fasting may be seen not by others but by your Father who is in secret; and your Father who sees in secret will reward you" (Matthew 6:16-18). These words effectively left in place the customary practice of Jewish fasting, but helped the disciples, ancient and modern, to understand that this act of devotion is only for God. It is not for individual acclaim. It is a personal act of joy and thankfulness, of sacrifice and release.

In the early church, individuals who were being initiated into the faith fasted like Jesus in preparation for their service to God. Fasting was a time to understand how much the initiates relied on God for their physical and spiritual lives. The body hungered and the discomfort and pain that resulted reminded the initiate of his/her need for food. The hunger focused the mind squarely on the provider of all good things. The individual's relationship with God came into stark relief and the benefits of this clarity directed and enhanced his/her ministry.

Fasting is a discipline that enables one to focus his or her prayers. For John Wesley, the most important reason for fasting was that it was a help to prayer and could be made more meaningful if it were combined with giving to the poor. "[John] Wesley was convinced that fasting, abstaining from food or drink, was a practice firmly grounded in the Bible. People in the Old Testament times fasted. So did Jesus and his followers, and Wesley saw no reason why modern Christians should not follow the same pattern."[10]

Regardless of how widespread the practice of fasting is in the Bible or religious tradition, it is not a common practice with North American Christians. Some people fast for health reasons but, by and large, Americans resist fasting.

Fasting is a sacrifice. It requires commitment, time, and physical discomfort. It is inconvenient and doesn't produce any visible benefit. In our task-oriented society, these realities mean that fasting is not valued and therefore not practiced. This is probably why Americans find fasting objectionable. We have lost our ability to practice most forms of spiritual discipline and fasting in particular. Art Simon describes this condition, "The problem is not that we've tried faith and found it wanting, but that we've tried mammon [the riches and bounty the world offers] and found it addictive, and as a result find following Christ inconvenient."[11]

A fast is not a diet. It is an effort at relationship building. A fast for spiritual purposes cannot be embarked upon without seeking God's assistance. Arthur Simon describes this dichotomy in his book, *How Much Is Enough*. "The heart will be filled. That is why Jesus asks us to hunger and thirst for the goodness of God. Doing so does not come naturally to us. On the contrary, it is natural for us to follow our own desires. So we begin always by inviting God to enter a heart that is instinctively unreceptive."[12] To prepare for a fast we need to work to make our hearts more receptive. Prayer will create a space big enough to receive God's grace and sustain you throughout the fast. Inner preparation for a fast of any duration requires that God be the focus.

To follow Christ, we are called to deny ourselves and take up our crosses and follow him (Matthew 16:24, Mark 8:34, Luke 9:23). Our reluctance to be uncomfortable for Christ deprives us of the intimate relationship that will feed us spiritually. If this is what we seek, fasting is an effective discipline— one worth considering.

A closer relationship with God is the ultimate purpose of fasting. "Fasting is a knife that cuts away superficiality, getting to the bone. Effective, because it is able to break up daily patterns upon which you have become so dependent. When those patterns of pleasure are removed, you are left with your own internal resources. If those resources are bankrupt, then during fasting, you will come face to face with a vacuum that only God can fill."[13]

We are not truly satisfied with the bread on our table because true satisfaction requires moving beyond our comfort zone. If you are stuck spiritually, you are probably too comfortable. You have drawn the line beyond which you are unwilling to go on your spiritual journey. A closer relationship with God will require you to make an effort, to make a sacrifice.

What does the word "sacrifice" bring to your mind? Does it mean giving something up for someone else? Does it mean doing something very difficult? If you sacrifice something, is it difficult and painful? Many people think that is what sacrifice means. But the word sacrifice means "to make holy." When you sacrifice something you make it holy. Fasting is a sacrifice of yourself. It is a way to become holy when you offer up your very essence for God's use.

If we are to discover the spiritual benefits of fasting, we must first know some basic rules. "Ignorance of basic rules can be dangerous, but if we follow a few simple guidelines there is little danger and much to be gained from a fast."[14]

God does not want us to injure ourselves in order to engage in this type of communion. Therefore, do not fast if you are ill, traveling, or under unusual stress. People with long-term, chronic illnesses should consult with their physician before undertaking a fast. "Some may not be able to fast from food (diabetics, for example), but everyone can temporarily give up something in order to focus on God. Even unplugging the television for a period of time can be an effective fast."[15]

When abstaining from food, particularly for the first time, people will find that they have less energy than normal. They may become irritable, have headaches, experience fatigue, or even weakness. This is normal. You should reduce your activity level. Do not engage in heavy physical labor. Avoid stress and stressful activities. Try to keep physical and emotional distractions to a minimum. You want to conserve your energy for the work at hand. Remember your focus is God and your relationship with God.

If you have never fasted before or for a long time, prepare your body in order to gain the greatest possible benefit from the fast. Reduce your food intake for a day or two ahead of time. A friend of mine only eats vegetables the day or two before she engages in a fast.

Richard Foster differentiates between fasts: normal, partial, and absolute. A normal fast is "abstaining from all food, solid or liquid, but not from water." A partial fast involves "a restriction of the diet but not total abstention." And an absolute fast means "abstaining from both food and water."[16] While none of these fasts has time lengths associated with them, one should not abstain from water for more than three days; any longer can cause serious harm to your body and its health.

When just starting out, work your way into it. Start with a 24-hour fast and drink only fruit juice (partial fast). A 24-hour fast means that you only miss two meals. Then fast for 24 hours the next week, drinking only water. You will want to do this several weeks in a row before embarking on a 36-hour fast (three meals). Fasting is not a race. Don't set too great a goal. You are looking for a long-term relationship and that takes a commitment.

Use the time you would have spent eating as a time of prayer and meditation. Notice that your body complains. Talk to God about your dependence on food. Notice that your body grows less uncomfortable with each effort. Keep a journal and note the changes in your body and in your outlook on the world.

Breaking your fast is as important as beginning it. Do not eat a large meal of fatty foods. Eat lightly. Vegetables and broiled chicken are good. The longer the fast, the more carefully you should begin and break it.

After you have undertaken a 36-hour fast for several weeks in a row, you may begin to consider a 40-day fast. Pray about whether this is the fast you are called to. Again, this is not a race. More is not necessarily better. However, people who have taken on the fasting discipline find that when they have moved past the six-month mark, their time begins to be more deeply meaningful to them. The body is not crying so loudly and you can better hear the voice of God in your fasting time.

"Six months after beginning the fast discipline, I began to see why a two-year period had been suggested. The experience changes along the way. Hunger on fast days became acute, and the temptation to eat stronger. For the first time I was using the day to find God's will for my life. Began to think about what it meant to surrender one's life."[17]

Fasting slows us down and allows us to listen for God's voice. Many people find that regular fasting changes the way they experience the world. They see their fellow humans as companions on life's journey. They learn to enjoy the bounty they are given more thoroughly, and are more ready to share with others.

Robert Farrar Capon wrote: "We should be careful about allowing abundance to con us out of hunger. It is not only the best sauce; it is also the choicest daily reminder that the agony of the world is by no means over. As long as the passion goes on, we are called to share it as we can—especially if, by the mere luck of the draw, we have escaped the worst pains of it. . . . Fast, therefore, until His Passion brings the world home free. He works through any crosses He can find. In a time of affluence, fasting may well be the simplest one of all."[18]

When we fast, we are changed. God changes us and directs in our ministry and mission. "If fasting is doing its work of liberating our focus from self-preoccupation, this will manifest itself in mercy and compassion toward those around us. We will be moved from within to give what we are receiving from God. . . . Our lives will be marked by concrete caring responses for others. Fasting must deal with reality. It does not skirt issues. It is not an interior escape"[19]

At the end of the fast, we find, like David, a rich feast. The meals we eat are flavored with the spice of limitation. The prodigal son had never had a better meal than the one he had after suffering with hunger. Our appreciation for what we do have is more profound and our senses more aware.

If we enter into a fast without a receptive heart, there is no room for God. This is a fast of cheap piety and unwilling participation as described in Isaiah 58:5.

> Is such the kind of fast that I choose,
> a day to humble oneself?
> Is it to bow down the head like a bulrush,
> and to lie in sackcloth and ashes?
> Is that what you call a fast,
> a day acceptable to the LORD?   (Isaiah 58:5)

A receptive heart will gain great nourishment and wisdom for a fast. It allows God to work within us to create the fast that God wants for us—a fast of humility, courage, charity, and justice.

> Is not this not the fast that I choose:
> to loose the bonds of injustice,
> to undo the thongs of the yoke,
> to let the oppressed go free,
> and to break every yoke? (Isaiah 58:6)

ENDNOTES

Introduction

1   "A Covenant Prayer in the Wesleyan Tradition," *The United Methodist Hymnal* (Nashville, TN: The United Methodist Publishing House, 1989), 607.

Chapter 1: Bread of Life

1.   "This Holy Mystery: A United Methodist Understanding of Holy Communion" was adopted by the 2004 General Conference of The United Methodist Church as an official interpretive statement of theology and practice in The United Methodist Church. It can be found in *The Book of Resolutions of The United Methodist Church, 2004* (Nashville, TN: The United Methodist Publishing House, 2005), 887.
2.   L. Shannon Jung, *Food for Life* (Minneapolis, MN: Augsburg Press, 2004), 26.
3.   Cathy C. Campbell, *Stations of the Banquet* (Collegeville, MN: Liturgical Press, 2003), 48.
4.   Jennifer Halteman Schrock, *Just Eating?* (New York: Church World Service, 2005), 5.
5.   *The United Methodist Hymnal* (Nashville, TN: The United Methodist Publishing House, 1989), 9.
6.   "This Holy Mystery," 892.
7.   Ibid.
8.   Jung, *Food for Life*, 52.
9.   "This Holy Mystery," 895.
10. Campbell, *Stations of the Banquet*, 165.
11. Jung, *Sharing Food* (Minneapolis, MN: Fortress Press, 2006), 134.
12. Ibid., 135.

13. Jung, *Food for Life*, 22-23.
14. Joetta Handrich Schlabach, *Extending the Table* (Scottsdale, PA: Herald Press, 1991), 214. This poem is part of the "Declaration of Conscience" which Kim Chi Ha, one of Korea's best-known poets, wrote while in prison.
15. Schrock, *Just Eating?*, 33.
16. Merriam-Webster Online Dictionary.
17. Jung, *Sharing Food*, 86-87.
18. Schlabach, *Extending the Table*, 64.
19. John Mogabgab, "Editor's Introduction," *Weavings* 7:6 (November-December 1992):2.
20. Schlabach, *Extending the Table*, 271.
21. Jung, *Sharing Food*, 31.
22. *The United Methodist Hymnal* (Nashville, TN: The United Methodist Publishing House, 1989), 621.
23. Schrock, *Just Eating?*, 5.
24. Jung, *Sharing Food*, 32.
25. Arthur Simon, *How Much Is Enough?* (Grand Rapids, MI: Baker Books, 2003), 168.

Chapter 2: Image of God

1. Arthur Simon, *How Much is Enough?*, 41-42.
2. William Barclay, *The Letters to the Corinthians* (Philadelphia, PA: The Westminster Press, 1975), 62.
3. Donna Scaglione, "Addicted to Being Busy," *Cape Cod Times*, September 27, 2004. http://archive.capecodonline.com/special/relax/addictedbusy27.htm
4. "What Americans Are Like," International Student and Scholar Handbook, University of Pennsylvania. http://www.upenn.edu/oip/iss/handbook/like.html#time

5. J. LaVelle Ingram, Ph.D., "Understanding American Worldview: Part III." http://www.lifeintheusa.com/culture/worldview3.htm

6. Joetta Handrich Schlabach, *Extending the Table*, 149.

7. Kathleen Zelman, MPH, RD, LD, "Slow Down, You Eat Too Fast," MedicineNet.com.
http://www.medicinenet.com/script/main/art,asp?articlekey+55932

8. Donna Scaglione, "Addicted to Being Busy," *Cape Cod Times*, September 27, 2004.
http://archive.capecodonline.com/special/relax/addictedbusy27.htm

9. "Take Control of Your Health." "US Food Industry Comes Under Scrutiny," *Washington Post*, March 16, 2003, and comment by Dr. Joseph Mercola.
http://www.mercola.com/2003/apr/5/food_industry.htm

10. Tershia d'Elgin, *What Should I Eat? A Complete Guide to the New Food Pyramid* (New York: Ballantine Books, 2005), has an excellent chapter on "Understanding the Nutritional Facts Food Label."

11. "Is It Possible to Love Overeating?" Intuitive Eating [blog], Melissa, March 29, 2007. http://returntoeatingintuitively.blogspot.com/

12. Julie Garden-Robinson, Food and Nutrition Specialist, North Dakota State University Extension Service, "Prairie Fare: Dinner with TV Influences Overall Nutrition," April 14, 2005.
http://www.ext.nodak.edu/extnews/newsrelease/2005/041405/03prairi.htm

13. An interview with Michael Pollan by David Roberts, May 31, 2006, Grist-Environmental News & Commentary.
http://www.grist.org/news/maindish/2006/05/31/roberts/

14. Alan Greene MD, FAAP, "Family Mealtime: All for One and One for All," April 1, 2005.
http://drgreene.org/body.cfm?xyzpdqabc=0&id=21&action=detail&ref=1906

15. "Is It Possible to Love Overeating?" Intuitive Eating [blog], Melissa, March 29, 2007. http://returntoeatingintuitively.blogspot.com/

16. Fitness Chronicles [blog], mcgheetraining, May 20, 2007. http://mcgheetraining.wordpress.com/2007/05/20/no-taste/

17. Weight-loss help: How to stop emotional eating, Mayo Clinic staff, December 1, 2005. http://www.mayoclinic.com/health/weight-loss/MH00025

18. "Stop Chocolate Cravings?" Yahoo! Answers. http://uk.answers.yahoo.com/question/index?qid=20070802095725A ADo7HQ

19. "Understanding Adult Obesity," WIN Weight-control Information Network. http://win.niddk.nih.gov/publications/understanding.htm

20. Lee Norman Miller, "History of food and agriculture," Agropolis-Museum, Montpellier Cedex, France, 1996-2006. http://museum.agropolis.fr/english/pages/expos/fresque/ la_fresque.htm

21. Schlabach, *Extending the Table*, 58.

22. The Capt/Sciontists of Soundz [blog], How Do I Overcome Over Eating and Obesity? How Do I Improve My Self Worth?, 29 April 2006. http://thecapt.blog-city.com/how_do_i_overcome_over_ eating_and_obesity__how_do_I_improve_.htm

23. Ibid.

24. Ibid.

25. Ibid.

26. Available at: http://www.annecollins.com/eating-disorders/statistics.htm

27. Carol Emery Normandi & Laurelee Roark, *Over It* (Novato, CA: New World Library, 2001), 6.

28. Ibid., 93-94.

Chapter 3: Hospitality – Sharing God's Bounty

1. Linda Green, "College Fellowship cooks up devotional," *United Methodist Reporter*, Section B, December 29, 2006.
2. Ibid.
3. Cathy C. Campbell, *Stations of the Banquet*, 73.
4. *The Interpreter's Dictionary of the Bible*, E-J, 654.
5. L. Shannon Jung, *Sharing Food*, 46.
6. Marjorie J. Thompson, *Soul Feast* (Louisville, KY: Westminster/John Knox Press, 2005), 133.
7. Ibid., 127.
8. Jung, *Sharing Food*, 39.
9. Sara Covin Juengst, *Breaking Bread: The Spiritual Significance of Food* (Louisville, KY: Westminster/John Knox Press, 1992), 37.
10. Henri J. M. Nouwen, *Reaching Out: The Three Movements of the Spiritual Life* (New York: Doubleday, 1975), 47.
11. Jung, *Sharing Food*, 49.
12. Joetta Handrich Schlabach, *Extending the Table*, 57.
13. Ibid., 94.
14. Ibid.
15. "Radical hospitality" is the act of extending community beyond the margins to those not served by the church. It is a commitment to just distribution of power and resources.
16. Rev. Dean Snyder, Foundry United Methodist Church, Washington, DC, Sermon: "A Working Faith: Our Wesleyan DNA," Sunday, September 21, 2003. http://www.foundryumc.org/sermons/9_21_2003.pdf
17. Mohandas Gandhi. http://www.hungernomore.org/quotations.html
18. Jung, *Sharing Food*, 50.
19. Bill Fentum, "Souper Bowl youth tackle hunger," *United Methodist Reporter*, Section B, January 26, 2007.
20. Jennifer Halteman Schrock, *Just Eating?*, 36.

21. Ibid.
22. Joetta Handrich Schlabach, *Extending the Table*, 174.
23. St. Francis of Assisi,
    http://thinkexist.com/quotation/for_it_is_in_giving_that_we_receive/
    14808.html

Chapter 4: Feasting and Fasting

1. The original Greek says, "And bring the fattened calf, sacrifice it, and
   let us eat and rejoice." "An Exegetical Tableau of the Parable of the
   Prodigal Son and the Elder Brother," a paper by Jeremy P. Roberts,
   November 16, 2006, 27.
   http://jeremyroberts.files.wordpress.com/2007/06/exegesis_
   prodigal_son_elder_bro.pdf
2. A PASSOVER HAGGADAH, A Guide to the Seder, United Jewish
   Communities and the Federations of North America. Available at:
   http://www.ujc.org/page.html?ArticleID=137175
3. Ibid.
4. Ibid.
5. Ibid.
6. Ibid.
7. Ibid.
8. Joetta Handrich Schlabach, *Extending the Table*, 294.
9. Chris Davis, pastor of Whitton Avenue Bible Church, Phoenix, AZ,
   Sermon: "Feasting on God," September 19, 2006.
   http://web.mac.com/simpleman52/iWeb/Chris%20and%20Rachel%2
   7s%20Website/Miscellaneous%20Sermons/FBE48D22-BF5C-4349-
   8C5F-1018A8321746.html
10. Charles Yrigoyen, Jr., *John Wesley: Holiness of Heart and Life* (New
    York: General Board of Global Ministries, 1996) copyright © 1996
    Charles Yrigoyen, Jr., 33.

11. Arthur Simon, *How Much Is Enough?*, 21.

12. Ibid., 165.

13. Ron Lagerquist, *Spiritual Fasting.* http://www.freedomyou.com/fasting_book/spiritual%20fasting.htm

14. Marjorie J. Thompson, *Soul Feast*, 80.

15. Christian Fasting - Spiritual Growth. http://allaboutgod.com/christian-Fasting.htm

16 See Richard Foster's chapter on fasting in *Celebration of Discipline* (San Franciso: Harper & Row, 1988), 49.

17. Thompson, *Soul Feast*, 85.

18. Schlabach, *Extending the Table*, 203. This passage comes from Robert Farrar Capon's book, *The Supper of the Lamb: A Culinary Reflection* (Garden City, NY: Doubleday & Company, Inc., 1969), 145.

19. Thomas Ryan, *Fasting Rediscovered* (New York: Paulist Press, 1981), 119.

BIBLIOGRAPHY

Anderson, George Christian. *Your Religion: Neurotic or Healthy?* Garden City, NY: Doubleday & Company, Inc., 1970.

Barclay, William. *The Letters to the Corinthians.* Philadelphia, PA: The Westminster Press, 1954.

Beckmann, David, and Arthur Simon. *Grace at the Table: Ending Hunger in God's World.* New York/Mahwah, NJ: Paulist Press, 1999.

The Book of Resolutions of The United Methodist Church, 2004, "This Holy Mystery: A United Methodist Understanding of Holy Communion," Nashville, TN: General Board of Discipleship of The United Methodist Church, 1995.

Buttrick, George Arthur. *The Interpreter's Dictionary of the Bible (Volume 2, E-J).* New York/Nashville, TN: Abingdon Press, 1962.

Campbell, Cathy C. *Stations of the Banquet.* Collegeville, MN: Liturgical Press, 2003.

d'Elgin, Tershia. *What I Should Eat? A Complete Guide to the New Food Pyramid,* New York: Ballantine Books, 2005.

Dole, Bob, George McGovern, and Donald E. Messer. *Ending Hunger Now.* Minneapolis, MN: Fortress Press, 2005.

Fentum, Bill. "Souper Bowl Youth Tackle Hunger." *United Methodist Reporter,* January 26, 2007, Section B.

Foster, Richard J. *Celebration of Discipline.* San Francisco: Harper & Row, 1988.

Green, Linda. "College Fellowship Cooks Up Devotional." *United Methodist Reporter,* December 29, 2006, Section B.

Juengst, Sara Covin. *Breaking Bread: The Spiritual Significance of Food.* Louisville, KY: Westminster/John Knox Press, 1992.

Jung, L. Shannon. *Food for Life.* Minneapolis, MN: Augsburg Fortress Press, 2004.

Jung, L. Shannon. *Sharing Food.* Minneapolis, MN: Fortress Press, 2006.

Kingsolver, Barbara, Steven L. Hopp, and Camille Kingsolver. *Animal, Vegetable, Miracle.* New York: HarperCollins Publishers, 2007.

Mogabgab, John. "Editor's Introduction," *Weavings* 7:6, November-December 1992.

Normandi, Carol Emery and Laurelee Roark. *Over It.* Novato, CA: New World Library, 2001.

Nouwen, Henri J. M. *Reaching Out: The Three Movements of the Spiritual Life.* Garden City, NY: Doubleday, 1975.

Outler, Albert C., ed. *The Works of John Wesley,* Vol. 1, Sermons I, 1-33, Nashville, TN: Abingdon Press, 1984.

Ryan, Thomas. *Fasting Rediscovered.* New York: Paulist Press, 1981.

Sack, Daniel. *Whitebread Protestants.* New York: St. Martin's Press, 2000.

Schrock, Jennifer Halteman. *Just Eating?,* New York: Church World Service, 2005.

Schlabach, Joetta Handrich. *Extending The Table.* Scottsdale, PA: Herald Press, 1991.

Simon, Arthur. *How Much Is Enough?* Grand Rapids, MI: Baker Books, 2003.

Thompson, Marjorie J. *Soul Feast.* Louisville, KY: Westminster John Knox Press, 2005.

The United Methodist Hymnal, Nashville, TN: The United Methodist Publishing House, 1989.

"The Wesleyan Graces 2," *The Book of Worship,* Nashville, TN: The United Methodist Publishing House, 1992.

Whitcomb, Holly W. *Feasting with God.* Cleveland, OH: United Church Press, 1996.

Yrigoyen, Jr., Charles. *John Wesley: Holiness of Heart and Life.* Nashville, TN: Abingdon Press, 1999.

ELECTRONIC RESOURCES

Capt/Sciontists of Soundz, The [blog], How Do I Overcome
   Over Eating and Obesity? How Do I Improve My Self
   Worth?, April 29, 2006. http://thecapt.blog-city.com/
   how do i overcome over eating and obesity how do i
   improve .htm/
"Christian Fasting - Spiritual Growth."
   http://www.allaboutgod.com/Christian-Fasting.htm/
Davis, Chris. "Feasting on God." A sermon presented to
   Whitton Avenue Bible Church, Phoenix, AZ , September 19,
   2006.
   http://web.mac.com/simpleman52/iWeb/Chris%20and%20
   Rachael%27s%20Website/Miscellaneous%20Sermons/FBE4
   8D22-BF5C-4349-8C5F-1018A8321746.html/
Erica. "Stop Chocolate Cravings?", Yahoo! Answers.
   http://uk.answers.yahoo.com/question/index?qid=200708020
   95725AADo7HQ/
Fitness Chronicles Blog, May 20, 2007.
   http://mcgheetraining.wordpress.com/2007/05/20/no-taste/
Gandhi, Mohandas.
   http://www.hungernomore.org/quotations.html/
Garden-Robinson, Julie. "Prairie Fare: Dinner with TV
   Influences Overall Nutrition." North Dakota State University
   Extension Service, April 14, 2005.
   http://www.ext.nodak.edu/extnews/newsrelease/
   2005/041405/03prairi.htm/
Ingram, J. LaVelle. Understanding American Worldview: Part III.
   http://www.lifeintheusa.com/culture/worldview3.htm/
Intuitive Eating Blog.
   http://returntoeatingintuitively.blogspot.com/
Lagerquist, Ron. "Spiritual Fasting."

http://www.freedomyou.com/fasting_book/spritual%20
fasting.htm/

Mercola, Dr. Joseph, *Take Control of Your Health,* "US Food
Industry Comes Under Scrutiny," *Washington Post,* March
16, 2003. http://www.mercola.com/2003/apr/5/food_
industry.htm/

Merriam-Webster Online Dictionary, copyright © 2005 by
Merriam-Webster, Incorporated. www.merriam-webster.com

Miller, Lee Norman. History of food and agriculture. Agropolis-
Museum, Montpellier Cedex, France. 1996-2006.
http://museum.agropolis.fr/english/pages/expos/fresque/la_
fresque.html/

The Passover Haggadah, A Guide to the Seder. United Jewish
Communities, The Federations of North America.
http://www.ujc.org/page.html?ArticleID=137175/

Roberts, David. "An Interview with Michael Pollan," *Grist:
Environmental News and Commentary,* May 31, 2006.
http://www.grist.org/news/maindish/2006/05/31/roberts/

Roberts, Jeremy P. "An Exegetical Tableau of the Parable of the
Prodigal Son and the Elder Brother." A paper presented to
Robert L. Williams, Ph.D., Southwestern Baptist Theological
Seminary, Fort Worth, TX, November 16, 2006. http://
jeremyroberts.files.wordpress.com/2007/06/exegesis_
prodigal_son_elder_bro.pdf/.

Scaglione, Donna. "Addicted to Being Busy," *Cape Cod Times,*
September 27, 2004. http://archive.capecodonline.com/
special/relax/addictedbusy27.htm/

Snyder, Dean. "A Working Faith: Our Wesleyan DNA." A sermon presented to Foundry United Methodist Church,
Washington, DC, September 21, 2003.
http://www.foundryumc.org/sermons/9_21_2003.pdf/

Statistics on Eating Disorders. http://www.annecollins.com/

eating-disorders/statistics.htm/

Weight-control Information Network.
   http://win.niddk.nih.gov/publications/understanding.htm/

"Weight-loss help: How to stop emotional eating." December 1,
   2005. http://www.mayoclinic.com/health/weight-
   loss/MH00025/

"What Americans are Like," International Student & Scholar
   Handbook, University of Pennsylvania.
   http://www.upenn.edu/oip/iss/handbook/like.html#time/

Zelman, Kathleen, "Slow Down, You Eat Too Fast,"
   MedicineNet.com.
   http://www.medicinenet.com/script/main/art.asp?
   articlekey=55932/

LEADER'S GUIDE
FOR
FOOD & FAITH

FAYE WILSON

LEADER'S GUIDE CONTENTS

Welcome to the Study!

This study is an invitation to explore our relationship with God through our relationship with the food that we eat. Author Wendy Whiteside writes, "Food is the basis of our physical lives, just as our relationship with God is the basis of our spiritual life." This study calls us to eat—spiritually and physically—and to reflect on how food strengthens our physical lives. I see us exploring five objectives.

We must:
• Reflect on our myriad experiences with food, especially in the context of our church life and faith journey;
• Review biblical scriptures which focus on the physical and spiritual aspects of sharing food;
• Renew our focus on the role of hospitality and sharing our food with each other in our faith walk;
• Remind ourselves to be thankful for our food by examining familiar and new table graces;
• Revitalize our commitment to living healthy lives through what we eat and through our fellowship with one another.

In this study we will first be called to think about how food and faith are inextricably linked in our own life experience. From remembering cake and coffee after church to recalling the variety

of Communion experiences that we have had, we will find ourselves thinking about how food has shaped our faith. We will
examine scriptures that teach us about hospitality, shared fellowship, and mission outreach—all in the context of breaking
bread together.

Second, we will be called to think about how we nourish our
body through food as we understand ourselves to be created in the
image of God. We ask ourselves the hard question: does our relationship with food overshadow our understanding of who God has
made us to be? The basic text author reminds us that the greatest
commandment, "love your neighbor as yourself" (Matthew 22:39)
includes the understanding that we are to practice self-love—a
choice that includes what we feed ourselves.

Third, this spiritual growth study challenges us not only to
use the food we have to feed ourselves, but also to feed our family,
our neighbors, our community. The essence of Communion is that
we are blessed to be a blessing to others. We eat spiritually so that
we may nourish the world. Hospitality, the sharing of God's bounty, is the response of every Christian. Ms. Whiteside writes:
"Somewhere under the cross we changed from strangers to guests."
And the cross experience further changes us to hosts and servants,
enabling us to extend hospitality to the homeless, the poor, the
lost, the broken.

Finally, the study calls us to understand the sacredness of
feasting and fasting for our own spiritual development. In examining biblical feasts as well as texts on fasting, we begin to fully comprehend the cycle of nourishment. In order to be fully satisfied and
fully nourished, we must sometimes turn away from physical food.
Whether we participate in a fast of the type that Daniel and his
comrades did—choosing to eat for nourishment rather than glut-
tony—or in a fast from all physical nourishment, the object of the
experience is to refocus on God's plan for our lives.

THE ROLE OF THE STUDY LEADER

This study guide is written for use in study settings: schools of Christian mission, United Methodist Women units, book clubs, and mission reflection groups. The leader's responsibility is to help establish an energetic learning climate. In every session, the leader reminds the group that each person's contribution is important, and that it is in the sharing of past experiences that new possibilities of hope and wholeness emerge for everyone in the learning group.

To that end, there are two important skills that a leader brings to the study process. One is to listen to the contributions of group members and link those experiences with the information in the study text. Listening is a whole body experience; the leader must be prepared to use positive oral feedback as well as to give brief words of thanks and affirming nods. Another important aspect of the listening process is to be aware of others who may put themselves down and not value their contributions, or those who may try to dominate the group sharing, or dismiss the contribution of others.

A second skill is to encourage the contribution of each member by organizing the lessons to tap into the variety of learning styles that participants use in the study process. The role of the study leader in this process is not to be a lecturer but to establish an atmosphere for maximum reflection on themes, exposure to new ideas, and expression of the learner's understandings of a topic. The leader should use every bit of space available (walls, ceiling, and floor) to share information. Desks and tables should be arranged so that the group can see the leader and each other. Charts, posters, and news clippings can adorn the walls. The leader should be attentive to the physical comfort and needs of the group. Can everyone hear? Are distracting sounds minimized? Is the temperature appropriately cool or warm for the physical body? Is there enough physical space so that people can move about?

One final comment: spiritual growth studies may elicit a variety of emotions. It is important to establish a covenant in the group process to allow people to share freely and to have their reflections held in sacred trust. There are times when the study process brings forth painful or difficult memories. Encourage the group to care for each other during this time.

LESSON PLAN

Each lesson is an opportunity to feast at a buffet. There are many menu options to choose from—from the experiences that are comforting and encouraging (such as remembering the best birthday party you ever had) to those that are full of fiber (reflect on a time when you did not nourish yourself well)—inviting you to clear away clutter and painful memories associated with food.

Each lesson has several common components (described below). This guide is just that, a guide to building the lessons using the various elements. Group leaders should feel free to organize the activities in a manner that feels most comfortable to them. Some components are combined in a lesson. And while each activity comes with a suggested time frame, more or less time can be given to an individual activity. The overall goal is to release creativity in each participant for the purpose of understanding the material.

The components are:

Biblical Reflection – Students will read scriptures that talk about food in the life of the faith community. From the manna and quails that the Israelites consumed in the wilderness to the eating of charbroiled fish after Jesus' resurrection, students will look at many concepts of food and faith as found in the scriptures.

Read Every Line – In order to get the most out of this study, students will be expected to read the basic text, *Food & Faith*. The exercises are designed to help learners delve into the text and link it to their own experiences in a variety of ways.

Worship – Students will have a time to acknowledge God's care for them and seek God's direction in their own lives and for people around the world. In a time when food is plentiful in some countries and markedly scarce in others, this study calls us to feed the hungry and bring the homeless poor into our homes and hearts.

With Thanksgiving – Saying grace is one of our first introductions to prayer. Many of us grew up saying, "God is great and God is good, and we thank Him for our food." There are an untold variety of table blessings available to us. All students will be asked to recall and write table graces for themselves and the class.

What's On My Plate– Students will use plates to think about their experiences, to create artwork, and to create fellowship within the class.

My Food Diary – Students will have a chance to write, to remember their various experiences in relationship to food—in church, in school, at home, on vacation. For some, the food diary will help them reestablish a healthy and loving relationship with the food that they eat and serve. For others, it will point the way for them to care more about those who hunger not only for food, but for love, for hope, for righteousness, for Jesus!

Abundant Table – Students will have an opportunity to feast by sharing food during each lesson. The abundance of this table does not come from the quantity of food offered or consumed. Instead, it comes from the ever-increasing richness of fellowship and reflection, of shared wisdom, and an expanding vision that there is food enough and faith enough for none to go hungry. The foods shared during this time should be healthy. Some should be unfamiliar and reflect the various cultures within The United Methodist Church.

Challenge – Often we have some negative memories associated with food and our faith journey. Students will be asked to reflect either on their own fractured experiences with food or those of others, with the goal of taking steps to mend the brokenness that exists within themselves, their own communities, or some aspect of the earth.

PREPARING TO LEAD THE LESSON

It goes without saying that the study leader should read the basic text thoroughly. When reading each chapter, do so with a pen and highlighters on hand (preferably a blue and a red pen to be sure that items stand out). Make notes in your book first—if a paragraph brings a song to mind, jot it down; if a statement doesn't jell with your thoughts, highlight that. If an author's story elicits a story of your own, jot down details of that story—right on the page. Write down scriptures that come to mind that may not be referenced in the text at all. Write down questions that come to mind or people with whom you should talk. (Ask Aunt Louise about the time that she had to cook for 50 people after church.)

Another step is to be in prayer about the study. Ask, and ask again, for God's guidance as you prepare to lead the sessions. As stated earlier, the leader needs the skills of facilitating, listening, challenging, and correcting—all in a caring manner. Ask God for wisdom, strength, and direction. Be thankful for the many wonderful experiences you have had with food (family holiday gatherings, trips to various countries, serving at church events, ministering in a food pantry or soup kitchen). Seek healing for any food-related memories that elicit painful thoughts.

A third step is to immerse yourself in food-related experiences. As early as possible, but at least a month in advance, be sure to watch a couple of cooking shows (Emeril, Rachel Ray, Bobby Flay, B. Smith). Take notes on how nutrition, food presentation, and hospitality are intertwined. Take notes on events at your church that include food. Help prepare a coffee fellowship and really pay attention to the conversation and the dynamics that occur during the preparation and the service of the meal. Pay attention to experiences in your everyday setting—meals with family members, lunch with work colleagues, official celebrations.

Scan magazines and newspapers for articles about food—both preparing food and people's experiences with food. Clip or photocopy those that are particularly interesting and place in a reading file for use in the class. Collect pictures of persons of all ages and nationalities involved with food: preparation, display, and fellowship. Use these for display in the classroom or make them available for study participants.

Another step in preparing to lead the lesson is to review all the music mentioned in the sessions. Music conveys both ideas and memories for you and the class. So go ahead; sing the hymns and graces that are part of the lesson plans. If any are unfamiliar to you, ask someone to play the unfamiliar songs for you. One caveat: for those who are teaching in regional and conference schools of mission, your group members are looking for material that they can use when they teach in their districts and units. Try to use music that is easily accessible.

That being said, I encourage you to draw on every resource that you have. Personally, I am a church musician who plays by ear. That fact, along with the wide variety of experiences I've had, means that I have had access to (in memory, in out-of-print songbooks, and in my file) a variety of songs. When teaching, I will use those songs that perhaps only I know, to enrich my class sessions. But I always will make sure to primarily use music that is readily accessible to the class.

SUPPLIES

The lesson plans call for use of a variety of supplies. (A supply list is given for each session and basic supplies are listed below.) Be sure to gather as much of this material as possible ahead of time. When teaching in regional and conference schools of mission, many supplies such as newsprint and assorted markers are provided for class use. However, it is always helpful for leaders to have their own tool kits of supplies that they use regularly in their lessons. (God bless the child that's got its own!)

The leader may communicate also with learners prior to the session to ask them to bring some items for use in the class setting. Here are some supplies that you will use throughout the study:

Bibles
Hymnals – *The United Methodist Hymnal*, *Global Praise* songbooks, camp songbooks
CD or cassette player
CDs and cassettes of songs related to food and faith
Paper plates (6 to 8 for each student)
Construction paper
Butcher paper
Paints
Paintbrushes
Straws or paint sticks
Glue
Glitter
Crayons
Masking tape

Magic markers
Clothesline
Clothespins
Index cards (4" x 6")
Scissors
Magazines (that feature food or people's relationship with food)
Reading file (copies of articles that relate to the themes of the study)

SESSION 1– BREAD OF LIFE

THEMES
- The joy of food—eating, memories of shared food
- The role of Communion in the life of the church, in our own lives
- Our commitment to extending the Communion table into the community
- Saying thanks for the food and fellowship that strengthen our lives

SESSION TIMETABLE
Opening Worship and Biblical Reflection (10 minutes)
What's On My Plate: Getting Acquainted (25 minutes)
Read Every Line (25 minutes)
With Thanksgiving and the Abundant Table (10 minutes)
My Food Diary (10 minutes)
Challenge (15 minutes)
Group Project Selection (10 minutes)
Closing Worship: "Always Remember—Jesus" Reader's Theatre (15 minutes)

SUPPLIES
Hymnals
Bibles
Nametags
Paper plates
Small paper or plastic plates
Napkins
Toothpicks or forks
Balls of yarn
Scissors
Hole puncher (individual)
Construction paper
Plain (typing) paper
Stapler and staples
Markers
Magazines
Index cards
Colored dots (four colors: i.e., green, blue, yellow, and red)
Copies of Reader's Theatre (if not in students' text)
Newsprint

LEADER PREPARATION
- Create an outline for the session. (You may use the one in the Leader's Guide. Review it thoroughly.)
- Create a "be sure to share" list of personal stories or illustrations to share during the various components of the lesson. (For example: if you have a story about a disastrous birthday party, you may want to tell it when explaining the "challenge" of linking food and faith.)
- Prepare foods for the Abundant Table.
- Assign (or plan to recruit) 13 volunteers to present the Reader's Theatre, "Always Remember—Jesus," at the end of

the lesson (11 disciples, 1 guest, and 1 narrator). Find or prepare music for use with the play, as directed.

- Be prepared to recruit a scripture reader and song leader for opening worship.
- Reread chapter one—Bread of Life.
- Bring foods for the Reader's Theatre (grapes, cheese, grape juice).
- Copy words for songs to be sung, observing copyright guidelines. Words may be printed on newsprint or projected via overhead or PowerPoint. Set up a supply table for use each day. Spread out supplies on a table for use in creating name tags, food diaries, and artistic renditions for What's On My Plate?
- Put writing prompt on newsprint (or PowerPoint) for the Food Diary and Challenge components.
- Put additional two verses of "In the singing" (*Global Praise* 2, #35) on newsprint.
- Arrange room (desks and chairs) in a semicircle for opening worship.
- Place an index card with a colored dot on it face down on every desk.

PLAN OF STUDY
Worship and Biblical Reflection

Sing: "As your children, Lord," *Global Praise 1*, #5 [tune: " Kum Ba Yah," *The United Methodist Hymnal*, #494]

Read scriptures: 1 Kings 17:8-16; 2 Kings 4:42-44; Matthew 14:13-21.

Reflection: Share a brief personal reflection on God's provision or read this meditation based on the biblical story of the widow of Zarephath: God provides! What a joyous assertion. The widow of Zarephath was down to a handful of meal and little oil in a jug and God provided. Nowhere does it say that the barrel was full of meal or that there was ever any more than a little oil in the jug. Yet the supplies did not run out. Trust that God has prepared the bread of life for you and that even if there is not plenty, there will always be enough. Praise God!

Testimony: Invite one person to share a one-minute witness to God's provision. (It's okay if no one volunteers. Just continue with the prayer.)

Prayer (unison): Most holy and gracious God, we are delighted to be in your presence and in the presence of each other to learn more about your holy Word and your will and your way for our lives. We are hungry not only for our daily bread but for your Spirit. May our study be a time for us to remember that we are yours and you provide for our every need. Feed us the bread of life that we may hunger no more. "Bread of heaven, bread of heaven, feed us till we want no more." In Christ's name we pray, Amen.

Sing: "In the singing," *Global Praise 2*, #35 [sing additional two verses with chorus].

Verse 3: *In confession, in forgiveness, in a heart made open, waiting*
In the greeting, in the sharing, in our lives, this blessing saves us.

Verse 4: *In our singing, in our praying, as we kneel before God, praising*
For the giver, for Christ's body, we find wholeness in the taking.

Getting Acquainted: What's On My Plate?

Welcome everyone to the class and invite them to make a nametag and participate in a reflection exercise. Give each person two paper plates. On one, have them create a nametag (direct them to items on the supply table). Ask participants to write their name in the center and decorate with glitter and drawings. Punch two holes in the plate about 4" apart; cut a length of yarn, 24" to 36", and loop through plates to wear around the neck.

With the second plate, ask class members to decorate it, dividing the plate into sections that depict the various commitments and duties that they have at this moment in their lives. Invite them to identify especially what they have given up or put aside to be part of this spiritual growth study.

After everyone has completed both tasks, have the students divide into groups, based on the color of the dot on the index card that was on their desk. In their groups, ask them to introduce themselves and share "what's on my plate." After all members have had a chance to introduce themselves, the leader should share with the groups "what's on my plate" and encourage the sharing to continue throughout the class.

Read Every Line

While remaining in the four groups, the leader should direct everyone's attention to the book. Assign each group selected pages to correspond with the following themes:

Communion – what are various forms of Communion? What approach is favored? What is a humorous Communion story? What is a most sacred moment?

Table Grace – what are familiar table graces? ("Johnny Appleseed"; "God is Great and God is Good.") Is saying grace at home, at church, at a restaurant, a family or personal practice? What is a humorous grace story?

Church Fellowship – inside the sanctuary (coffee klatches, pancake breakfasts) – what do we enjoy about church meals? What's the downside? What contributions do people make to the fellowship? Share a humorous moment.

Church Fellowship – outside the sanctuary (church camp,

women's retreat) – what kinds of foods are part of the camp experience (i.e., s'mores)? What do we enjoy or dislike about the outdoor food experience? What is a strong spiritual experience that happened during a camp or retreat? Name a funny moment.

Ask each group to recruit a recorder to take notes about what is shared and a reporter to share the team's thoughts. The leader should be prepared to add personal anecdotes related to the theme after each team has shared. *[Collect index cards at end of exercise for use in next lesson.]*

With Thanksgiving

Sing the song, "The food we now partake," *Global Praise 2*, #57. Give out index cards and ask everyone to write a table grace. It can be one that the person creates or one that is part of her or his family experience.

Abundant Table

After the graces have been written, ask that they be brought to the Abundant Table and place them amidst the food choices. Invite everyone to take a sample of the foods that are offered for the day.

My Food Diary

As people finish sampling the foods, direct them to the supplies table again and ask them to make a food diary. Staple together five blank sheets of paper, making a cover using construction paper. (Encourage them to decorate the covers with artwork and pictures they cut from magazines.)

Post writing prompts on newsprint or project from a laptop. Encourage all students to write in their food diary reflecting on one or more of the following prompts:

Food(s) we always have at our church suppers (peas and dumpling soup);

How food and fund-raising are linked in our church or home (mission trips, building fund drives);

All-time favorite foods;

Strangest foods ever consumed (snails, frog legs, rattlesnake, alligator).

Challenge

As people conclude journaling in their food diaries, ask them to find a partner and share some of what they've written. After everyone is paired, give the following assignment. Food is known for bringing people together. Recall a time, however, when food "fractured" the fellowship. Share a story from personal experience or say: "*A woman in our church always volunteers to prepare the meal when we have out-of-town guests. She only wants to cook by herself; she makes it clear that she is in charge of the meal. But because of her lone ranger spirit, she has difficulty recruiting people to serve. So the meals for our guests are always late and haphazard. She complains to the pastor that no one will help her. We need to heal this fractured fellowship.*" Talk to your partner about fractured fellowships in your church or home experience. Brainstorm solutions and remedies. If time permits, ask for two volunteers to give a one-minute witness about a fractured food fellowship AND a possible remedy.

Group Projects

Share the following group projects and invite classmates to select one on which they are willing to focus. Even though small group work is built into every session, the group projects are designed to have people use their best skills and their own interests to share with the class in the final session.

PROJECT: PUPPET THEATRE (ART AND DRAMA)

Participants will make puppets (using paper plates and craft sticks/straws) to create a play about food and faith. For example, the team might explore the significance of Communion in the lives of Christians. The team could illustrate a first Communion experience, Communion in other cultures, or a humorous Communion experience, etc.

PROJECT: BIBLE GALLERY (ART AND THEOLOGY)

Participants will create either a mural or individual posters depicting various biblical themes about food and faith. Refer to the scriptures in the study or use some familiar ones: feeding of the 5,000 (Matthew 14:13-21); Jesus frying fish on the beach (John 21:1-12); Abigail bringing a food peace offering to David (1 Samuel 25).

PROJECT: SINGING GRACES FOR CHURCH FELLOWSHIP (MUSIC)

Many of us grew up singing the graces, "Be Present at Our Table, Lord" and "Johnny Appleseed." The group will be asked to create three to five brand new, singable, table graces for use in our homes and churches.

PROJECT: HOSPITALITY HOTEL (GUIDELINES WITH GRACE)

What makes everyone welcome at the table? The group will be asked to create and/or compile a minimum of "Ten Tips" for great hospitality. Using the backdrop of a hotel motif, they will be asked to create a mini-play to present what makes their hotel the heart of hospitality. The team should bring in biblical references and themes that highlight hospitality (i.e., Isaiah 58:6-12).

Assignments for Session 2:
1. Read the remainder of the book, especially chapter two— Image of God.
2. Think about the Group Project options that were presented and select one.
3. Write in food diary about any food that you really savored in the past 24 hours.

<u>Closing Worship:</u> Use the Reader's Theatre to conclude the session.

Always Remember—Jesus! (Reader's Theatre)

<u>Introduction</u>

This play takes place in the upper room in Jerusalem. The year is 34 CE, one year after Jesus met with his disciples for a last meal before his death. The time is Passover.

The eleven remaining disciples, along with special guest Matthias, join together for the evening meal. Peter is the host for the Passover meal and greets each disciple as he enters.

The disciples are seated around one long table or two long tables formed in a V-shape.

<u>Cast of Characters</u>

Peter (host/narrator for the meal)	Matthew
Philip	Matthias
Thomas	John
James (son of Alphaeus)	Bartholomew
Thaddeus	James
Simon the Zealot	Andrew
Narrator	

<u>Staging</u>
The table is set with cups, clusters of grapes, cheese cubes, and flat bread. Peter is the only disciple present in the room. Have other cast members seated or standing to one side in the order in which they enter the room.

Music

Play in the background the song "Always Remember Jesus" by Andrae Crouch, (*Finally* album), and reduce to near mute as narrator speaks. *Finally* is an out-of-print album but the music may be found online. Check amazon.com for copies available for resale.

If this music is not available, consider asking a volunteer pianist to play and record an assortment of Communion hymns ("In the singing," *Global Praise 2*, #35; "As your children, Lord," *Global Praise 1*, #5; "Fill My Cup, Lord," *The United Methodist Hymnal* #641; "One Bread, One Body," #620).

Or have the choir sing "Let Us Break Bread Together," *The United Methodist Hymnal*, #618.

Narrator:	The year is 34 CE. The day is Passover. Peter is waiting to greet the other disciples who are coming together to eat the Passover meal and to remember Jesus.
Peter:	It's hard for me to believe that it's already one year since my Lord and Savior died. I am looking forward to seeing the other guys—it has been a busy year. Most of all, I'm looking forward to remembering Jesus—who he is and all that he did when he lived among us.

[SIMON AND THOMAS ENTER]

Simon:	Peter, it's me Simon. Thomas is with me. Are we the first to arrive?

[JAMES AND JOHN ENTER]

James: Simon, you and Thomas may be first ones to step through the doorway but John and I are right behind you.

Narrator: The Passover or last supper with Jesus was one in which he gave new meaning to the traditional sharing of the bread and cup. Many things have happened in the lives of these disciples since they were together here in this room with Jesus.

[PHILIP AND MATTHIAS ENTER]

Philip: James, John—is that you? I was hoping that we'd all be able to make it.

Simon: I'm over here—and Peter, strong Peter, is here to greet us all.

[BARTHOLOMEW AND ANDREW ENTER]

Narrator: Today the disciples have gathered to reminisce about their last time with Jesus and talk about their personal experiences throughout the year.

[JAMES (SON OF ALPHAEUS)—REFERRED TO AS JAMES (A), THADDAEUS, AND MATTHEW ENTER]

Peter: Brothers, my brothers, it is good to be united once more around this Passover table and in this room, this room that holds many memories. We have been scattered to the east, west, north, and south, proclaiming the gospel. We have been faithful in the service of our Lord.

Simon: I tell you it has not always been easy. Jesus told us to be good examples for anyone who would ask about our ministry. But that has been difficult.

Thomas: That has been true for me, too. After I first doubt-ed that Jesus had risen and then I saw him alive, I double-vowed to serve him wholeheartedly. But when I was out there preaching, I wanted to return home—back to Jerusalem.

Peter: My brothers, I do understand these feelings. I've had a few myself. But the Lord commanded us to be faithful—and there was NO promise that it would be easy.

Andrew: I'm just glad to be with all of you. I know that I will be encouraged by our fellowship.

Peter: Speaking of fellowship, let's sit down around the table [**EVERYONE SITS**] and break bread as Jesus taught us.

[**EVERYONE IS SEATED:** Choir or soloist sings "I Come with Joy," *The United Methodist Hymnal*, #617, [or sings one verse of "Let Us Break Bread Together," #618]

Peter: [LIFTING UP THE BREAD AND CUP] Praise to you O Lord our God and King. You have created the fruit of the vine and have caused the earth to yield wheat for our bread. In the name of Jesus, Amen.

All: In the name of Jesus, Amen!

James (A):   Peter, thank you for making the arrangements for this meal. And it's good to have Matthias, who was chosen to take the place of Jude, here with us.

Matthias: Thank you for choosing me and accepting me in this ministry. Although I was not one of the original twelve disciples, I was one of the 70 that the Lord commissioned. I am honored to serve.

James: It is indeed a blessing to be chosen. John, do you remember just four years ago when we were fishing with our father Zebedee?

John: Yes, I do. Jesus came right up to us and asked if we wanted to be fishers of men. It seemed a strange request. But it was even stranger that we just dropped our nets and went with him. Even though our father needed our help with the boat, we were compelled to follow Jesus.

James: Sometimes I miss the sea. I miss the smell of the water, the fish jumping in the net—and the steady income!

Philip: Yes, I know what you mean about the money—but if we hadn't left all to follow Jesus we would be lacking in one very important thing—peace of mind. Now we are doing God's will and that is most important.

Thaddaeus: Sharing this meal is so important. And I remember that meal when all the people followed us. It was more than 5,000 people that were fed with five loaves and two fish. I will never forget that miracle. From that moment on, I no longer doubted the power of Jesus.

Bartholomew: Philip, I am so glad that you introduced me to Jesus. If you recall, I didn't think anything GOOD could come out of Nazareth. Boy, was I wrong! I will never forget the moment I saw Jesus, or, more importantly, when Jesus saw me. I was a doubter and doubt still hampers my ministry. Brothers, please pray for me about that.

Thomas: Bartholomew, you know I understand what it means to doubt. I will never forget when Jesus told me to put my fingers in his palms, and put my hands in his side. That made a believer out of me. But I want people to believe in Jesus on the basis of my testimony. And sometimes they doubt my experience.

Peter: Matthew, you have been strangely quiet all evening. Is everything okay?

Matthew: It is not because I'm not glad to be here. There just is an ocean of thoughts going through my head. When James and John were talking about leaving their nets, I thought about when I left my job to follow Jesus. And, like James, sometimes I miss the income (being a tax collector was a peachy job). In fact, my desire for wealth did not just disappear overnight—but with God's help, I am committed to spreading the gospel.

James (A): We have had some losses but, oh, what a great gain we have all had!

ALL: Say that again, James!

James (A): As we break bread tonight and reflect on the call, let us remember that we have yet to experience all the joy that Jesus promised to us.

Thaddaeus: You are so right. Remember our Lord said, "All a person must do is love me, keep my word, and he will find FAVOR with me and my Father." Having that favor is more important than gold. We must continue to be faithful.

Simon: I have a confession to make. I wasn't known as Simon the Zealot for nothing. I wanted Jesus to set up a kingdom here on earth and I was prepared to defend it with my sword and my life. But now I see how wrong I was. If his kingdom was just here in Jerusalem, it never would have spread to the ends of the earth as it needed to. I pray that God will continue to give us strength to go everywhere with the gospel, no matter the cost.

Peter: Yes, all of us gave up much at the time of our call. But may we always remember what we've gained.

And may this meal, as the Last Supper was for Jesus, be a time to prepare for the challenges yet before us. Let us drink once again, and eat once again and REMEMBER that time when our Lord commanded us to do this OFTEN in remembrance of him. Let us eat and drink and remember.

[DISCIPLES EAT AND DRINK]

ALL: Jesus, in our partaking of this cup and eating of this bread, we renew our commitment to your CALL on our lives and accept all of its challenges. In your name, we pray, AMEN!

Music: Play the song "Always Remember Jesus" or sing "Leaning on the Everlasting Arms," *The United Methodist Hymnal*, #133, as characters exit the stage.

SESSION 2 – IMAGE OF GOD

THEMES

- Who do we see when we look in the mirror?
- How do we perceive our bodies as temples of God?
- What are our struggles with food and health?
- How can we "get over it"—our obsession with food and weight?

SESSION TIMETABLE

Opening Worship (5 minutes)

Get Acquainted: All Things in Common Grid (15 minutes)

Small Group Food Exercise (30 minutes or more)

Biblical Reflection (10 minutes)

Read Every Line (15 minutes)

With Thanksgiving (15 minutes)

What's On My Plate: Self-Portraits (10 minutes)

My Food Diary (10 minutes)

Abundant Table (10 minutes)

Challenge (15 minutes)

Closing Worship (10 minutes)

Group Project Work (10 minutes)

SUPPLIES

Hymnal or song sheets

Bibles

Nametags

Paper plates

Construction paper

Markers

Scissors

Stapler

Magazines
Hand mirrors
Full-length mirror (if possible)
Copies of All Things in Common grid
Small bottle of olive oil
Tissues
Snacks, food for the Abundant Table
Copy of the poem, "The Party" by Paul Laurence Dunbar
World map with markers

PREPARATION

- Create an outline for the session. (You may use the one in the Leader's Guide. Review it thoroughly.)
- Create a "be sure to share" list of personal stories or illustrations to share during the various components of the lesson.
- Prepare foods for the Abundant Table.
- Be prepared to recruit a scripture reader and song leader for opening worship.
- Reread chapter two—Image of God.
- Copy words for songs to be sung, observing copyright guide lines. (See notes in Session 1.)
- Set up a supply table.
- Put writing prompt on newsprint (or PowerPoint) for the Food Diary and Challenge components.
- Arrange room (desks and chairs) in a semicircle for opening worship.
- Place an index card with a colored dot on it face down on every desk.

PLAN OF STUDY

Welcome

Greet students as they enter the classroom. Tell them you are looking forward to hearing their thoughts on the upcoming chapter.

Worship

Sing: "Many Gifts, One Spirit," *The United Methodist Hymnal,* #114.

Read scripture: 1 Corinthians 3:16.

Reflection: Talking to the one in the mirror. Michael Jackson recorded a song called "Man in the Mirror," saying that he was talking to that man and telling him he had to change his ways. Today we will hold up a mirror to our lives and ask God (while looking at our reflection) to see if we are doing all that we should and could be doing to live in God's image. If you have a mirror in your purse or pocket, I invite you to take it out and simply look inside it. If you don't have a mirror, I have a couple that I am circulating. (If you have a full-length mirror, say the following: Or feel free to get up and study your reflection in the full-length mirror against the wall.) For one minute, let us see God in ourselves. (Call everyone back to his/her seat.)

Prayer (unison): Lord, we have looked in the mirror and fallen in love. We are in love with ourselves; thank you for creating us. We are in love with your generosity; help us to live and give in the same way. Help us to show the love that you've shown us to ourselves and to each other. In Christ's name we pray, Amen.

Sing: "Jesus Loves Me," *The United Methodist Hymnal,* #191 (verse 1 and chorus).

Getting Acquainted

Give everyone an All Things in Common sheet (see end of

session) and ask each person to find people to sign in a block (one name for each block). Try to complete as many blocks as possible. (Leader could have prizes for students who got every block filled in or the students who had the most boxes filled in.)

Bring group back together. Read aloud each box and ask those who signed in that particular box on anyone's sheet—OR could have signed that box—to stand if they are able, (say, "it's morning aerobics time") or wave their hands (if they cannot pop up and down). After all boxes have been claimed, ask the class for popcorn (quick) observations: i.e., surprised at the number of people who eat chitlings, Mexican food, etc.

Small Group Food Exercise

Choose one of the following two exercises: (1) Can you do it? Can you eat food that comes from within a 200-mile radius? Plan a menu for ONE WEEK of EACH SEASON to see if you could eat food originating from your geographic area. (2) Plan a treasure hunt. Split into teams of three to four and go on an excursion to a local supermarket. Go to the produce and meat section to discover where the food is grown, farmed, or raised. When you return from your excursion, lay out a world map, and place markers on each place in the world our food comes from.

When the project you have chosen is done, discuss this. If we have food from all over the world readily available in our supermarkets, why are there so many people without food in this world? Are the countries growing our food also countries that are feeding their people well?

Biblical Reflections

Have the class gather into groups again. Give each group these scriptures, ask them to look them up, read them, and write down what they believe the scriptures say about our being made in God's image and taking care of our bodies and our spirits: Genesis 1:24-31 (are we to be vegetarians?); 2 Samuel 9:1-7; Matthew 22:36-38; Acts 2:42-47; 1 Corinthians 6:19. Have each group give a one-minute report on their findings.

Read Every Line

Discuss chapter two of the text. Highlight how we fail to take care of ourselves by not eating in community, eating more than we should, and being so busy that we fail to make choices based on good nutrition. Stephen Covey wrote in his book, *The Eighth Habit*, that it is important to "subordinate" our taste to nutrition, thus giving our trillions of cells (not just our taste buds) what they need to thrive. Ask the class to share their thoughts on the chapter as you review it with them. Tap into their strengths by creating a list on newsprint of things that help and hinder the fueling of soul and body.

With Thanksgiving: Sandwich Swap

Sing the Johnny Appleseed grace: "O, the Lord's been good to me; and so I thank the Lord, for giving me the things I need, the birds and the bees and the appleseed; the Lord's been good to me." Hand each person an index card and invite each one to try his/her hand at writing a grace that can be sung to a familiar tune such as the chorus of "Jesus Loves Me."

Next, ask everyone to gather around the supply table and use materials (construction paper, markers, etc.) to make a favorite sandwich (i.e., use red paper for tomatoes, green paper for lettuce, tan paper for bread, brown paper for beef). Tell students that once their sandwich is made, they are to staple their grace to it. Have them return to their seats and put their names on the back.

Have the students, without leaving their seats, begin to circulate the sandwiches around the room. Have students read the grace and write on the back of the sandwich what kind they think it is. After three minutes, return sandwiches to the original owners. Invite them to share what people thought their sandwich was and what it really was. All persons should close their sharing time by reading aloud their grace and thanking God for their favorite sandwich.

What's On My Plate?

Give each person a paper plate and ask her/him to create a self-portrait that accentuates each one's best features. Share that many people have become accustomed to disparaging their bodies and their faces (too fat, too full, too many scars). Remind the group that God rejoices over us with singing as he rejoiced over the daughter of Zion (Zephaniah 3:14-17). If permitted to use the wall, ask everyone to hang her/his portrait on it.

My Food Diary

Post these writing prompts on newsprint or project from a laptop. Give students time to begin writing in their food diary on one or more of the following topics. If you have time, you may read (or ask for a volunteer) the monologue "Throwing Away Food in My Body" (see end of lesson) prior to persons reflecting in their food diaries.

The Consciousness of Chewing – describe the flavor, texture, and experience of eating a cookie, an apple, popcorn, or almonds. Confess – using the concept of "no shame, no blame—admit and move forward," write a statement to yourself confessing any bad food decisions or poor health choices and promise to move toward a healthier life style.

Abundant Table

Upon completion of journaling (or while journaling), encourage students to visit the Abundant Table and take a sample of the goodies that have been prepared. Remind them to read the table graces that have been placed there or to use the table grace that is attached to their favorite sandwich (from earlier exercise).

Challenge

Healing the fractured food fellowship: Ask the class to initiate conversations at lunch or supper with persons who are not taking the class about how to handle a "food pusher," that woman at church who gives you a second helping when you have refused, or the neighborly gentleman who pouts if you don't have three helpings of his barbecued ribs. Or ask them to initiate conversations about how to reach a person who treats her/his body like a trashcan when it comes to food.

Assignments for Session 3

4. Review the remainder of the book, focusing especially on chapter three.
5. Invite students to bring unique tasting items to the Abundant Table.
6. Recruit a person to read/recite Paul Laurence Dunbar's "The Party."
7. Have group members commit to a Group Project option.
8. Ask Hospitality group if they could be ready to share in Session 3.
9. Recruit volunteers to read aloud selections from "Cultural Jubilee Moments" (end of session plan for chapter four).

Closing Worship

Arrange chairs in a circle for the closing worship.

Sing: "Slow down, you eat too fast" (tune: "Feeling Groovy")
Slow down, you eat too fast; you need to make the flavor last—just Take your time, as you lift your spoon

Sip your soup—and you'll feel groovy.
Slow down, you chew too fast; don't let this moment pass—pick
Up your fork and take a small bite
Put it back down—and you'll feel groovy.
Take the time to gather 'round; it's not your last meal in town, no
It's a time to for us to share
At the table—and to feel groovy.

Say an Affirmation. Ask for five volunteers to stand in front of a full-length mirror or hold a hand mirror and say this affirmation: "Mirror, mirror, on the wall, I am the fairest of them all. I am comely and beautiful this I know, because the Bible tells me so. I'm a child of God, made of clay, coming to love myself more each day. I pledge this day, from now and now on, I will eat good things— and show this temple love! Mirror, mirror on the wall, I am the fairest of them all."

Healing Circle: Circulate a vial or small container of a mildly scented oil (such as olive oil). Ask each person to anoint and pray for the person to the left. Let all be in a meditative spirit. Turn to the person on one's left and ask if they desire healing for their bodies and their relationship with food. If the person says "yes," anoint them with oil and say, "I pray for you; may God answer your prayers."

If the person says "no," ask if they would like anointing to continue their quest for wholeness in every aspect of their body, and ask if you may anoint them and pray, "Thank you God for creating _____ in your image." Continue around the circle until everyone who desires to be has been anointed.

Prayer (unison): God, thank you for every good gift that you have given us. Help us to lay aside every weight and every sin that so easily besets us. Help us to choose wise nutrition so that we may love and honor the bodies that you have so lovingly given us. May we pause and taste the food we eat. May we pause and fuel our bodies for gracious service to others. May we pause and share our food and fellowship with each other. May you meet every need that we have so that our longing for food provides us with the healthy bodies we need. In Christ's name we pray, Amen.

Sing: "I Am Thine, O Lord," *The United Methodist Hymnal,* #419.

All Things in Common

Find out what things you may have in common with your classmates. Ask classmates to sign in the box if they have participated in the activity. Ask classmates to choose only one box to sign. Have only one name per box.

Eaten alligator meat	Fasted for more than 48 hours	Tried the South Beach Diet	Lost and kept off more than 50 lbs. for a year or more	Loves hot and spicy foods [such as jalapeno peppers]
Supervises the kitchen in their church	Likes to eat hard fruit (pears, apples)	Been to a wedding reception [in the past three months]	Likes Mexican food	Taken cooking classes
Loves to eat chitlings, hog maws, & pig feet	Made a Thanksgiving dinner for more than 35 people	Had an unusual food experience not named on this sheet What????	Loves to eat muskrat or deer or squirrels	Has a garden and grows vegetables such as beans, carrots, asparagus
Loves macaroni and cheese	Used the Cabbage Soup Diet	Hates going grocery shopping	Been on Weight Watchers	Likes Italian food
Has more than three sizes of clothes in their closet	Considers chocolate a vegetable (because it comes from a bean)	Loves peanut butter & jelly sandwiches	Does not eat vegetables	Thinks mashed potatoes is the best food ever

Throwing Away Food in My Body

I am not a trashcan. So why do I treat my body as such? I confess: I throw away food in my body. Last night it was my daughter's leftover potatoes. I don't even like potatoes, but I hate to see food go to waste. I hate to throw food down the garbage disposal, so I toss it away—in me.

Last month my doctor said I had gained 10 pounds since my last physical. I think it's more. Why? I don't move as quickly as I used to. I am buying larger-sized clothes. I try not to catch a glimpse of myself in a mirror. I am not happy with the physical or spiritual me.

Yes, I treat myself as a trashcan. I gobble down my food at lunch. I stuff a doughnut in my mouth that's left in the employee lunchroom as I pass through to take a paper to a colleague. It's there for anyone to eat, so why do I not savor it? Why do I snatch it up, put it all in my mouth at once—and gulp? Because that's what you do to a trashcan. I mean, you don't tear a sheet of paper up in bits and pieces, one at a time, to throw it into a trashcan (actually, I should recycle that paper). No, I ball it up and throw it away quickly.

But that is not how I should treat my body. Today, I stop—and think—and listen to God's love for me through God's word. My body is a temple, not a trashcan. My body is my shelter—not a shack. So I will treat my body well. I will treat my spirit better. I will honor myself and love myself by eating those things that are good, by sharing a meal with others and by savoring the food and the fellowship. I am not a trashcan. I will not treat myself as such anymore.

SESSION 3 – HOSPITALITY

THEMES
- Exploring the biblical understanding of hospitality

- Remembering when we have received and have given hospitality
- Affirming hospitality as a key component of mission service
- Preparing ourselves to serve our neighbors

SESSION TIMETABLE
Opening Worship (5 minutes)
What's On Your Plate: Guess – Who's Coming to Dinner? (20 minutes)
Biblical Reflection (10 minutes)
Read Every Line (15 minutes)
With Thanksgiving (15 minutes)
Abundant Table (15 minutes)
My Food Diary (5 minutes)
Challenge (15 minutes)
Closing Worship (10 minutes)
Group Project Work (10 minutes)

SUPPLIES
Hymnals or song sheets
Bibles
Paper plates
Construction paper
Markers
Scissors
Stapler
Magazines
Snacks, food for the Abundant Table

PREPARATION
- Prepare foods for the Abundant Table. Try to have foods from

different cultures and experiences. Some suggestions include: pickled pig feet; chitlings; tripe; smoked oysters; artichoke hearts.

- Create an outline for the session. (You may use the one in the Leader's Guide. Review it thoroughly).
- Create a "be sure to share" list of personal stories or illustrations to share about practicing and giving hospitality.
- Be prepared to recruit a scripture reader and song leader for opening worship.
- Reread chapter three— Hospitality.
- Copy words for songs to be sung, observing copyright guide lines. (See notes in Session 1.)
- Make sure the supplies table is adequately stocked.
- Put writing prompt on newsprint (or PowerPoint) for the Food Diary.
- Arrange room (desks and chairs) in a semicircle for opening worship.
- Place an index card with a colored dot on it face down on every desk.

PLAN OF STUDY

<u>Worship</u>

Gather in a circle for worship.

Sing: "The church is like a table," *Global Praise 2*, #102.

Read scripture: Matthew 22:1-10 (Wedding Banquet).

Testimony: Invite one person to share a one-minute witness to their experience of hospitality, either giving or receiving it. (It's okay if no one volunteers. Continue with the prayer.)

Prayer (unison): "A Covenant Prayer in the Wesleyan Tradition," *The United Methodist Hymnal*, #607.

Sing: "I'm gonna live so God can use me," *God's Mission,*

God's Song, #1.

<u>What's On Your Plate?: Guess – Who's Coming to Dinner?</u>

Set the stage for this exercise by hearing the reciting of the poem, "The Party" by Paul Laurence Dunbar. Next, share the story of Oprah Winfrey's 2005 Legends and Young'uns Luncheon (January 2005, *O magazine*). She invited nearly 100 persons whom she admired, young and older, for their contributions to society. In a particularly poignant moment, she had the young'uns read a poem entitled "We Speak Your Names," to the legends, the older persons who were trailblazers in their respective areas.

Have students decorate a paper plate with their name in the center. Around the edges put the names of five people with whom they'd like to have dinner. Then have them gather in assigned groups and share with each other the people with whom they would like to break bread.

<u>Read Every Line and Biblical Reflection</u>

Review with the group the author's experience in southwest Hungary. Ask if they have ever been lost and someone out of the blue helped them out. The author mentions that the cross on the business card made the difference. For some it may be the fish on their car or even a Masonic emblem. Allow time for one or two persons to share.

Ask the group to list places where they see hospitality being shared (either given or experienced). Hopefully they will go beyond the everyday hospitality to include ministry at homeless shelters, prison ministry, clothes closets, and other forms of mission outreach. Ask if there are people whose church youth groups participate in the Souper Bowl of Caring or have specific hospitality ministries (i.e., have a Soup Kitchen).

Invite the group to name any barriers they may experience to extending or receiving hospitality. For some, they may feel their home isn't good enough; for others, their home may be so fine they are reluctant to have people over. Then there are situations that are complex and reaching out in ministry or receiving can be a struggle. Revisit the story of the woman in Lesotho who had been waiting to show hospitality to her guest at the same time the guest was trying NOT to be at her home for a meal.

The author mentions that we are keenly aware of the need for Christ's presence in times of extreme joy or crisis. Share the story "Stone Soup Wedding" at the end of this session; ask others if they have had any "stone soup" experiences in their lives.

Also, review the scriptures mentioned in chapter three (Matthew 25; 1 Peter 4:9; Romans 12:13) and share what the Bible teaches about hospitality.

Finally, invite the group that worked on the guidelines for hotel hospitality to present their project to the class.

With Thanksgiving (15 minutes)

Share this information with the class—the focus so far has been on recalling table graces and writing new ones. In this session, class members are asked to affirm the importance of setting a table where everyone is welcome. The work of Glide Memorial United Methodist Church (San Francisco) found an even broader audience when the movie, "The Pursuit of Happyness," hit the big screen in 2007. America saw the church's commitment to feeding the poor and sheltering the homeless, always in a spirit of offering a helping hand "up"—rather than kicking someone while he is down.

Another example of hospitality can be found in the work of United Methodist Women units all over the world. The UMW unit in Wesley Temple United Methodist Church, Salisbury, Maryland, holds an annual international dinner. Not only do unit members and their guests get a chance to expand their taste buds, they also have a chance to give to mission through the donation for the meal. Grace United Methodist Church, St. Alban's, New York, United Methodist Women's primary fundraiser is a salad luncheon, again to raise money for mission projects such as the outreach to women imprisoned at Riker's Island.

Invite the class to meet in their groups and share stories of hospitality in the context of church fellowship. Allow time for one story from each group to be shared with the entire class.

Abundant Table

Invite people to taste foods that may be totally new to them (see list). Class members may be asked in previous communication to bring something to share. If time permits, allow volunteers to share one or two of the vignettes from "Hospitality Cultural Moments."

My Food Diary

Encourage students to write in their diary any cultural hospitality experiences they have had. Perhaps they have broken bread with a church whose members are from a different ethnic persuasion. Perhaps they have journeyed to other countries (and to other states) where they were offered fried bread or smoked bear meat (as they might experience when visiting some communities in Alaska). Perhaps they have had an experience where they were denied food because of the color of their skin. Encourage them to use the stories from Sandra Ruby and others as a model for writing their life stories in their food diary.

Challenge

How do we deal with the greedy and the need in the house of God? There are some church members, Bible-toting believers, who still want to make every celebration, every fellowship, about them.

If they bring a pie, they want that announced: "Sister Lillie brought the peach cobbler!" If a youth in the choir is applauded for great grades, then her grandson who lives 3,000 miles away must be recognized as well.

Has anyone heard about church kitchen cliques? Sometimes there are one or two persons who are the kitchen committee. They only accept food prepared by their friends. Even when others volunteer to help, they refuse the help or disparage their efforts: "They just don't know how we do things." Sometimes this disregard for a sister or brother member can lead to those members feeling they have nothing to share and they feel unwelcome in the house of God.

On the other side of the coin are the ones who seem to never be able to keep a job, save their money—and they appear to come to church with the hand out. "Gimme, gimme," is their refrain. How do we interrupt the constant need for a spotlight? How do we help without being an enabler? Ask class members to pair up to share war stories and recommendations for change.

Closing Worship

Sing: "For everyone born," *Global Praise 2*, #34.

Read: (volunteer) "I once read an article about one woman's struggle to know what to do when approached by a homeless person or someone on the street asking for money to buy milk for a baby. She also worked in a homeless shelter once a month and at times felt stressed by the overwhelming need that she met at every turn. She wrote this prayer to help her through: "God, _____, is your child and I care about her/his welfare. So if there is something I can do, please help open that door for me. But at this point, I don't see that open door so I am entrusting _____ to your care. Bring the right person(s) into her/his life so that hopefully she/he can have a different life than the one she/he has now, if that is your will. Amen." According to the article, in praying that prayer, she was able to stay emotionally and spiritually strong, and found doors opening for herself and the people whom she served.

Prayer: Invite everyone to consider if there is someone in her/his life for whom this prayer is appropriate. Invite everyone, as a group, to pray this prayer, inserting the name of the person(s) whom God has laid upon their hearts.

Sing: "Jesu, Jesu," *The United Methodist Hymnal*, #432.

Assignments for Session 4

10. Review the remainder of the book, focusing especially on chapter four.
11. Add a reflection to the Food Diary about a topic selected earlier in the class.
12. Remind everyone that the remaining Group Projects are to be shared in Session 4.
13. Invite anyone who wishes to do so, to observe a fast— skipping dinner and breakfast.

Group Project Work

Allow time where possible for the remaining three groups to finish their presentations.

Stone Soup Wedding (as told to author by Ann Evans)

Ann approached her wedding day with both joy and a bit of sadness. It was a great day but both she and Steve were broke. But she sent out the invitations anyway, largely by email: "Come celebrate our special day with us. Meet us at the Foundation Hall for the ceremony and we'll have wine and munchies afterwards."

Then the sister network went to work. Debbie plopped down an amazing amount of money for steamed shrimp. Jean called others and said, "Bring soda, bring crackers, bring cheese." Someone made three cakes. Keri ran to the mill outlet and grabbed bolts of slinky materials and made simple but festive tablecloths. Someone else ordered a bunch of balloons. And so it was that on her wedding day, in the company of 300+ family and friends, with children waving peacock feathers and scattering the good wishes of spring over everyone, Ann and Steve joined their lives.

Remember the story called "Stone Soup" when a stranger came to town and set a pot over a fire in the town square, poured in water, put in a stone, and proclaimed that he was going to make stone soup? As the stone and water heated, he periodically tasted the water and said, "this is good but would taste better if I had ..." calling out various ingredients such as a carrot, an onion, a turnip. Eventually, with the help of the townspeople, he produced a wonderful soup that all shared. Ann and Steve's wedding could simply have been the most elegant and meaningful stone soup wedding ever.

Cultural Hospitality Moments

Alaska – Thom White Wolf Fassett was the general secretary of Church and Society for several years. Once, while traveling with a team to Alaska, he led us in a period of orientation as we prepared to meet native peoples who are members of the Alaska Missionary Conference. He shared that one of the most important things to do is to accept with grace and thanksgiving the food that would be set before us. He explained that he was a vegetarian but if he went in someone's home and they had prepared a meal that had beef or fish, he would eat what was shared with him.

Cambodia – I have never witnessed before or afterwards greater hospitality than was shown to me and to our mission team by Marilyn and Joseph Chan. Joseph and Marilyn had managed to escape the scourge of Pol Pot and eked out an existence in the refugee camps in Thailand. While there, through the faithful and caring hospitality of church workers, Joseph accepted Jesus Christ and became a faithful servant. In fact, Marilyn and Joseph became the first official United Methodist missionaries in Cambodia.

For him, there was no status associated with being a missionary; he was there to serve. And he served a group of Americans over and over again as we struggled to adjust to the heat, the different time zone, and the painful genocide history of Cambodia to which we were being introduced. I pray that I, too, can serve anyone who comes my way in that manner.

Gabon (fish in a basin) – "Let's go explore the marketplace," Vivian urged me. We were at a conference in Gabon and things were not going well according to my US standards of comfort. I did have a room. Several people did not and had camped out in the hotel lobby following a 12-hour flight from New York. So, during the break, we ventured forth. As we wandered, a gentleman began talking to us. He kept referring to us as "my sisters from America." I confess. I clutched my purse a little tighter.

He urged us to come meet his friends. "We are Senegalese but we work here in Gabon," he said. The street was open (no dark alleys) so we went with him. (I was praying the entire time.) In a few minutes, we were seated on crates having a conversation with six gentlemen. "We are about to have lunch," our host said. "Please share with us." From nowhere a huge basin filled with rice, peas, fish, carrots, and eggplant appeared. Everyone—but Vivian and me—dipped in with his hands. Without missing a beat, our host found us spoons. Despite being warned to not eat from street vendors, my girlfriend and I dug in. We tasted the sweetest carrots. The eggplant was tender, the fish flaky. And we laughed the afternoon away—and never felt a moment of sickness. Thank God for the hospitality.

Japanese Tea Ceremony – I know it was set up just for tourists but I sat eagerly watching the intricate ritual of the ceremony. The pot was warmed and rinsed. The tea was carefully steeped and artfully poured. It was not just the warmth of the tea that drew me in but the ritual—the great care with which the beverage was prepared. May I learn to lovingly prepare food and drink in a similar manner for all those with whom I come in contact.

St. Albans, New York – On the other end of the phone was one of my religion studies professors. "I have a student who has an internship in New York but she needs housing. Could you possibly help her?" Living in a parsonage with two young daughters, I didn't have a spare room but we made space. And thus Monica Leon-Chung entered my life in 1987 and remains a good friend today.

One Saturday morning she said that she wanted to cook breakfast for us. As we gathered at the table, she placed a bowl of scrambled eggs with a breakfast meat mixed in: sautéed squid. My three-year-old daughter whispered loudly to me: "Mommy, am I eating a monster?" " No," I assured her," it's just something different for me." And so Monica introduced me to a wonderful new taste; but I never did share her liking for tripe (cow stomach) and the smell of it cooking was quite strong and lingered seemingly for days. No problem—I wanted her to be at home, and she was.

SESSION 4 – FEASTING AND FASTING

THEMES
- Rejoicing through shared food and fellowship
- Feasts from around the world
- Fasting for a Spiritual Feast
- Historical review of fasting in the United Methodist tradition

SESSION TIMETABLE
Opening Worship (5 minutes)
With Thanksgiving (15 minutes)
Read Every Line and Biblical Reflections (25 minutes)
What's On Your Plate (20 minutes)
Abundant Table (15 minutes)
My Food Diary (5 minutes)
Challenge (15 minutes)
Closing Worship (10 minutes)
Group Project Work (10 minutes)

SUPPLIES
Hymnals or song sheets
Bibles
Items for Abundant Table – cookies, crackers, fresh fruit
Markers
Pens
Paper plates

PREPARATION
- Create an outline for the session. (You may use the one in the Leader's Guide; review thoroughly.)
- Create a "be sure to share" list of personal stories or illustrations to share during the various components of the lesson.
- Reread chapter four—Feasting and Fasting.
- Copy words for songs to be sung, observing copyright guide lines. (See notes in Session 1.)
- Arrange room (desks and chairs) in a semicircle for opening worship.
- Have adequate supplies handy.
- Place the writing prompt for the Food Diary exercise on newsprint or project via PowerPoint.

PLAN OF STUDY

Worship

Sing: "Just a Closer Walk with Thee," *Songs of Zion*, #46, verse 1.

Pray (unison): Most holy and gracious God, every good gift comes from you. We give thanks for the abundance of food and fellowship that most of us know. Teach us to follow your ways and deny ourselves so that we may draw closer to you. In Christ's name we pray. Amen.

Sing: "Just a Closer Walk with Thee," *Songs of Zion*, #46, verse 2.

With Thanksgiving

Have the remaining three groups to present their work to the class. Allow time for group members to ask questions of the group as to how they see their projects being used in church or other arenas.

Next, using stories at the end of the lesson, share cultural feast experiences. (You could ask for volunteers to read aloud.) Ask if someone in the class has a cultural experience that she or he would like to share.

Read Every Line and Biblical Reflections

Present a summary of chapter four, highlighting the biblical texts that focus on feasting and fasting, and sharing the Wesleyan experience of fasting. When talking about feasts, brainstorm with the group the different kinds of feasts that they are a part of (Thanksgiving, Kwanzaa karamu, wedding receptions, baby christening dinners).

If any class members participated in the voluntary fast from Session 3, invite one or two persons to share what it was like. Also, ask if there are class members who regularly fast or may have participated in a fasting experience such as the Daniel Fast (eat only fruit, vegetables, and water for a week or two). Request that reports follow the one-minute witness (brief) model.

What's On Your Plate?

Share that Stephen Covey, author of *The Seven Habits of Highly Effective People,* is an advocate of fasting. He wrote in his book, *The Eighth Habit,* that he believes in the "efficacy and wisdom of occasional fasting, wherein you miss a meal or two for the purposes of providing rest to the whole digestive process and also for the cleansing" (p. 332).

Ask everyone to take a paper plate and write an invitation to a fast or a feast to someone they know; give a scripture or rationale from class. Upon completion, fold paper plates in half, staple, and place in a basket (or on a table). Mix them up and return a plate to each class member. Ask several people to share the message they received and how it touched them.

Abundant Table

Gather around the table, remember the Passover experience, and eat and share the food.

My Food Diary

Ask the group to take 3 to 5 minutes to make notes in their food diary about how the study *Food & Faith* has changed them. Ask them to make note of any thing new they will try or new decisions they have made in reference to food, faith, and fellowship as a result of the study.

Challenge

When it comes to church feasts (or those at work), many people struggle with making wise food choices and eating within the recommended guidelines for calories. Have the group review the monologue, "I Throw Food Away in My Body" in Session 2. Have participants individually list strategies to maintain the fellowship in church settings while practicing wise nutrition and then share their ideas with other classmates.

Closing Worship
    Sing: "Sent out in Jesus' Name," *Global Praise 2*, #113.
    Say a Litany: "We Speak Your Name." (Float the role of the leader, beginning with one person and moving to the left for each leader voice.)
Leader: To everyone born, there's a place at the table.
All: Come over here where the table is spread and the feast of the Lord is going on.
Leader: _____ (name of person to the left), I have learned from you as I examined my own ideas about food and faith.
All: _____, we speak your name and pray that you will be joyful in your eating.
Leader: _____ (name of person to the left), I pray that you and everyone else in the circle will find a place to receive hospitality.
All: _____, we speak your name and pray that you will be blessed by the food that you partake.
Leader: _____ (name of person to the left), I pray that you will find a place to extend hospitality; may God enlarge your territory; may you bring the homeless poor into your circle of friends.
All: _____, we speak your name and call on God to make you a Wesleyan warrior (worker) for justice and peace in your community.
Leader: _____ (name of person to the left), have not our hearts burned within us as we learned from the scripture what the Lord requires of us?

All: _____, we speak your name and ask that you join us on the journey to health and wholeness, to service and commitment.

All: Food and faith – may we be continually nourished by the word of God and the friendship of God's people. Amen!

Sing: "Sent out in Jesus' name" (Enviado soy de Dios), *Global Praise 2*, #113.

Cultural Jubilee Moments

Kwanzaa – Kwanzaa is a cultural holiday created for African Americans. It does not have to be observed exclusively by African Americans. In fact, many of the seven principles discussed on the seven days between December 26 – January 1 are applicable for community building and creating hospitable environments.

One component of Kwanzaa, the Karamu, observed on January 1st, is the feast for family and friends. It is designed to elicit the creativity of the community. All foods served are to be prepared by participants. (Store bought items are discouraged.) I remember one Kwanzaa when it seemed as if the table would break under the generous offerings that everyone brought. We feasted and feasted. Finally, when we were beyond satiety, we sat down and played games.

But lo, there was another donation to the table as one family came in a bit later. Whoosh! Winston Peter's curry chicken disappeared as if no one had had anything to eat. Were we greedy? Perhaps, a bit. I think more so because we knew the wonderful taste of Mr. Peter's food and we knew his great generosity of spirit; we just wanted to inhale both.

Steamboat Alley in Singapore

Shirley Wu encouraged a tired group of mission travelers, saying that we needed to have a unique eating experience while visiting church projects in Singapore. I was so weary from nights of insomnia that it was hard to think that I was actually going for dinner on a boat.

As we entered the restaurant from the street, I was definitely puzzled. But I followed gamely as we were seated around a circular table with a bubbling pot of liquid in the middle. She explained to us how we would get a plate of various meats and vegetables (sliced and diced) and using our chopsticks we would cook them in the broth. And we were urged to be sure to "drink some broth." Pushing aside fears, I got right down to the business of cooking my food in the savory liquid. (I never dipped out any to drink, though.) I chased a shrimp or two around and around in the broth—and lost a few vegetables along the way. But in the end, the experience was worth it—the laughter that floated up as we unschooled Americans tried something new helped forge a stronger traveling community.

Potlatch – this is a ceremony of giving (for which families save for many years) as a way to show appreciation for members of the community. In its earliest form, it was said to be a display of wealth. In modern day practice, it is a display of generosity, where all can come and celebrate (a wedding, the birth of a child, a graduation) and those who come actually are the big receivers. One might say that Oprah's Big Give encompasses elements of the potlatch. What is shared is meant to be passed on; the potlatch's purpose is to nurture generosity and security in the community.

INTERGENERATIONAL SESSION – FOOD & FAITH

[Three-hour session for a mixture of ages.]

THEMES

- Remember that we are created in God's image
- Reflect on the role of wise nutrition in our physical and spiritual development
- Recall the significance of Communion in the Body of Christ
- Review the meaning of hospitality and explore the ways in which it is practiced in faith settings
- Remember our table graces that we learned as children and the ones that we say as adults
- Reconnect with our vision of health and wholeness through food and faith for God's community

SUPPLIES

Hymnals
Bibles
Nametags
Paper plates
Small paper or plastic plates
Napkins
Toothpicks or forks
Balls of yarn
Scissors
Hole puncher (individual)
Construction paper
Plain (typing) paper
Stapler and staples
Markers
Magazines
Index cards

Colored dots (four colors: i.e., green, blue, yellow, and red)
Copies of Reader's Theatre (if not in students' text)
Newsprint

LEADER PREPARATION

- Create an outline for the session. (You may use the one in the Leader's Guide. Review it thoroughly.)
- Create a "be sure to share" list of personal stories or illustrations to share during the various components of the lesson. (For example: if you have a story about a disastrous birthday party, you may want to tell it when explaining the "challenge" of linking food and faith.)
- Prepare foods for the Abundant Table.
- Recruit a pianist to play hymns and songs during the session.
- Recruit a helper to assist with putting up newsprint, projecting words on PowerPoint.
- Plan to recruit 13 volunteers, or assign class members, to present the Reader's Theatre: "Always Remember—Jesus" (p. 137) - (11 disciples, 1 guest, and 1 narrator). Find or prepare music for use with the play as directed.
- Be prepared to recruit volunteers to read scriptures, share experiences, serve as readers.
- Bring foods for the Reader's Theatre (grapes, cheese, grape juice).
- Copy words for songs to be sung, observing copyright guidelines. Words may be printed on newsprint or projected via overhead or PowerPoint. Set up a supply table.

PLAN OF STUDY
Worship and Biblical Reflection (10 minutes)

Sing: "As your children, Lord," *Global Praise 1*, #5 [tune: Kum Ba Yah].

Read scriptures: 1 Kings 17:8-16; 2 Kings 4:42-44; Matthew 14:13-21.

Reflection: Share a brief personal reflection on God's provision or read this meditation based on the widow of Zarephath—God provides! What a joyous assertion! The widow of Zarephath was down to a handful of meal and a little oil in a jug and God provided. Nowhere does it say that the barrel was full of meal or that there was ever any more than a little oil in the jug. Yet the supplies did not run out. Trust that God has prepared the bread of life for you and that even if there is not plenty, there will always be enough. Praise God!

Testimony: Invite one person to share a one-minute witness to God's provision. (It's okay if no one volunteers. Continue with the prayer.)

Prayer (unison): Most holy and gracious God we are delighted to be in your presence and in the presence of each other to learn more about your Holy Word and your will and your way for our lives. We are hungry not only for our daily bread but for your Spirit. May our study be a time for us to remember that we are yours and you provide for our every need. Feed us the bread of life that we may hunger no more. "Bread of heaven, bread of heaven, feed us 'til we want no more."[2] In Christ's name we pray, Amen.

Sing: "In the singing," *Global Praise 2*, #35 [sing additional two verses with chorus].

Verse 3:   *In confession, in forgiveness, in a heart made open, waiting*
      In the greeting, in the sharing, in our lives, this blessing saves us.

Verse 4:   *In our singing, in our praying, as we kneel before God, praising*
      For the giver, for Christ's body, we find wholeness in the taking.

Getting Acquainted: What's On My Plate?

Welcome everyone to the class and invite them to participate in a reflection exercise. Give each person a paper plate and ask her/him to decorate it, dividing the plate into sections that depict the various commitments and duties that they have at this moment in their lives. Invite them to identify especially what they have given up or put aside to be part of this study session. Encourage them to pair with another student and discuss what's on their plate.

Presentation: Bread of Life (Intersection between food and faith)

In this first hour, lead the group to examine their experiences with food in the context of the church (table graces, food fellowship, experience of Communion). Ask the group to continue to work in groups of two or three and discuss the following questions or statement. (Allow a minimum of five minutes per statement.)

The Table is Spread!!!

Identify the various kinds of food and fellowship events at your church (give suggestions such as pancake breakfasts, coffee klatches, potluck suppers). What do you enjoy about church meals? What's the downside? Share a humorous moment.

Saying Grace

Think about blessing our food for a moment. What are familiar table graces? ("Johnny Appleseed"; "God is Great and God is Good.") Is saying grace at home, at church, or at a restaurant, a family or personal practice? What is a humorous grace story (i.e., when Uncle George prayed for 15 minutes over the Thanksgiving dinner and everything got cold).

Creative Moments

Sing familiar table graces ... "Be Present at Our Table, Lord," "Johnny Appleseed," "God is Great."
Learn a new grace: "The food we now partake," *Global Praise 2*, #57.
Write a table grace (spoken or sung).
Seek volunteers to share a grace with the entire group.

Planning

Recruit 13 persons to present "Always Remember—Jesus" (p. 137); give them 5 minutes to review the material. You may appoint a 14th person to be the director.

Taking Communion

Communion – what are various forms of Communion that you've experienced? What approach do you favor?
What is a humorous Communion story? What is a most sacred moment?

Creative Moment

Have a presentation of "Always Remember—Jesus" (p. 137). Get the class involved by singing the hymns as directed.

Write in My Food Diary

Tell the group that throughout the session they will be encouraged to think about their experiences with food, in and outside the church. Ask them to set aside a section in their notebook or get several sheets of paper and fold them together to make a food diary. Tell them that throughout the session they will be given a story prompt and they will be asked to write in their food diary as another way of thinking about their relationship with food and faith.
Prompt #1: What are the three strangest foods that you've ever eaten? That you've ever heard of someone eating?

Challenge (Adults)

Share this thought with the group. Food is known for bringing people together. (Think Christmas and Thanksgiving dinners, graduation parties, wedding receptions.) But all is not necessarily smooth and calm at the table. Share a story from personal experience or say: *"A woman in our church always volunteers to prepare the meal when we have out-of-town guests. She only wants to cook by herself; she makes it clear that she is in charge of the meal. But because of her lone ranger spirit, she has difficulty recruiting people to serve. So the meals for our guests are always late and haphazard. She complains to the pastor that no one will help her. We need to heal this fractured fellowship."*

Have the class divide into groups of four persons and recall a time when food fractured the fellowship. Talk about fractured fellowships in your church or home experience. Brainstorm solutions and remedies. Ask volunteers to share solutions they have come up with for healing fractured fellowships.

Drama: Puppet Theatre (children)

Have some volunteers work with children to make puppets (use paper plates and craft sticks/straws) to create a play about food and faith. For example, the children could talk about how they take Communion or they could talk about their favorite foods to eat at church potluck suppers.

Presentation: Image of God

Give everyone a paper plate. Make sure there are adequate markers and crayons for use by all students. Tell the story of the little girl who was drawing in class one day. She was working so intently her teacher asked her: "Sally, what are you drawing?" Sally replied, "a picture of God." Not wanting to discourage her, but feeling she needed to inject some reality into the picture, the teacher replied, "but honey, no one knows what God looks like." Without looking up, Sally replied: "They will when I get through."

Remind the class that we are created in the image of God. Ask them to take a paper plate and draw self-portraits, being sure to accentuate their best features (eyes, beard, smile, heart).

Creative Moments

Listen to the monologue, "Throwing Away Food in My Body" (p. 154).

Write in My Food Diary

Post these writing prompts on newsprint or project from a laptop. Give students time to begin writing in their food diary on one or more of the following topics.

• The Consciousness of Chewing – describe the flavor, texture, and experience of eating a cookie, grapes, almonds, or an apple.

• Confess – using the concept of "no shame, no blame—admit and move forward," write a statement to yourself confessing any bad food decisions or poor health choices and promise to move toward a healthier life style.

Challenge (Adults)

Read aloud to the group the scriptural passage: Isaiah 58:6-12. Remind the students that earlier they looked at an example of fractured fellowship in the body of Christ. Have them review their notes and conversation and create a "big ten" list of what makes for great hospitality. Encourage creativity by asking students to create a Five Star Hospitable Hotel. What represents the heart of hospitality?

Art Gallery (children)

Provide materials to children and ask them to make their favorite sandwich. Adults may help some children write the name of the sandwich on the construction paper.

Art Gallery (adult)

Encourage adults with artistic ability to opt out of journaling and use the time to create individual posters depicting various biblical stories about food and faith. They can draw pictures of Jesus cooking on the beach, feeding the 5,000, turning water into wine. They can draw a picture of the widow of Zarephath with the oil, jug, and flour barrel.

Abundant Table

Allow time for a stretch break. Invite people to stop by the Abundant Table and sample the goodies (both new and familiar foods).

Creative Moments

To gather the group back together, distribute the "All Things in Common" worksheet (p. 153) and have them find people who have similar experiences with food. Or you may project it from a PowerPoint projector and still have the class participants discuss with their classmates things that are in common or different.

Presentation: Hospitality

Discuss various components of hospitality as outlined in the text. Share the vignettes that describe cultural hospitality (p. 162).

Presentation

Present a summary of chapter four, highlighting the biblical texts that focus on feasting and fasting, and sharing the Wesleyan experience of fasting. When talking about feasts, brainstorm with the group the different kinds of feasts that they are a part of (Thanksgiving, Kwanzaa karamu, wedding receptions, baby christening dinners).

Be sure to ask if there are class members who regularly fast or may have participated in a fasting experience such as the Daniel Fast (eat only fruit, vegetables, and water for a week or two). Hear from a couple of volunteers. Request that reports follow the one-minute witness (brief) model.

<u>My Food Diary</u>

Encourage students to write in their diary about any cultural hospitality experiences they have had. Perhaps they have broken bread with a church whose members are from a different ethnic persuasion. Perhaps they have journeyed to other countries (and to other states) where they were offered fried bread or smoked bear meat (as they might experience when visiting some communities in Alaska). Perhaps they have had an experience where they were denied food because of the color of their skin. Encourage them to use the stories from Sandra Ruby and others as a model for writing their life stories in their food diary.

<u>Closing Worship</u>

Sing: "Just a Closer Walk with Thee," *Songs of Zion*, #46, verse 1.

Pray (unison): Most holy and gracious God, every good gift comes from you. We give thanks for the abundance of food and fellowship that most of us know. Teach us to follow your ways and deny ourselves so that we may draw closer to you. In Christ's name we pray. Amen.

Sing: "Just a Closer Walk with Thee," *Songs of Zion*, #46, verse 2.

ABOUT THE AUTHORS

Wendy Whiteside

Wendy Whiteside is a communicator with a BA in Theater and an MA in Communication. More importantly, she has a lot of experience communicating with others. Whether her job was packing lightning rods or teaching about the root causes of hunger, Wendy has been sought out as a communicator. Currently, Wendy is an Associate General Secretary of the General Commission on Christian Unity and Interreligious Concerns.

Wendy spent 15 years as staff of the General Board of Global Ministries, the mission arm of The United Methodist Church. Most recently she oversaw print, web, multilingual, video, and audio communications for Global Ministries. Prior to that she spent 10 years with the United Methodist Committee on Relief where she was responsible for communication. She directed the hunger ministries program, and coordinated many of the UMCOR projects receiving money from the Advance for Christ and His Church.

Wendy is a preacher's kid from Missouri and has worked for the church in many different positions since college. She spent eight years as the Associate Director of the Office of Creative Ministries where she nurtured and strengthened ecumenical ties within the state of Missouri. Over her career, she has hosted radio shows and written articles for print and web.

Faye Wilson

Dr. Wilson is coordinator of communications and parent/community outreach for the Wicomico County Board of Education. She co-produces a monthly cable program, *Working Together for Children*, and oversees the website.

Dr. Wilson is a member of Mt. Zion UMC (Quantico, MD) where she works in music ministry, serves as vice-president of her church's United Methodist Women's unit, and as coordinator for Zeal of Zion (praise dancers). She also directs a 35-voice community choir, Voices United, composed of singers from Mt. Zion, Friendship UMC (Wetipquin), New Missionary Baptist (Quantico), and St. Luke UMC (Hebron).

Formerly on the staff of The United Methodist Church's mission agency for 21 years, she developed many mission education resources, led seminars, and visited mission projects in the 50 US states and more than 20 countries. She continues to teach in schools of Christian mission.

She holds a BA in religion studies (Wilson College), a master's in theological studies (Drew Theological School), a master's in journalism (New York University), and a doctorate in adult education (Columbia University).

ADDITIONAL RESOURCES

Los Alimentos y la Fe
Wendy Whiteside
Guía para Líderes: Faye Wilson
(Food & Faith, Spanish translation)
M3048-2009-01
$7.00

일용할 양식과 신앙
웬디 와잇사이드
지침서: 페이 윌슨

(Food & Faith, Korean translation)
M3049-2009-01
$7.00

Food, Faith, and Me
by Kelly C. Martini
M3055-2009-01
$8.00

"Food Security," *Response* magazine, March 2009.
R3022-2009-01
$2.75

http://gbgm-umc.org/umw/foodfaith/

Available from: Mission Resource Center
800-305-9857
www.missionresourcecenter.org